OUR WORLD

EXPLORE THE NATURAL WONDERS OF **PLANET EARTH**

PaRragon

Bath · New York · Cologne · Melbourne · Delhi
Hong Kong · Shenzhen · Singapore · Amsterdam

This edition published by Parragon Books Ltd
in 2015 and distributed by

Parragon Inc.
440 Park Avenue South, 13th Floor
New York, NY 10016
www.parragon.com

This edition © Parragon Books Ltd 2012–2015
© Original edition by Editorial SOL 90 S.L.

This edition produced by Jollands Editions
Cover design by JC Lanaway

ISBN 978-1-4723-8054-8

Printed in China

Based on an idea by Editorial SOL 90

Cover images courtesy of istock

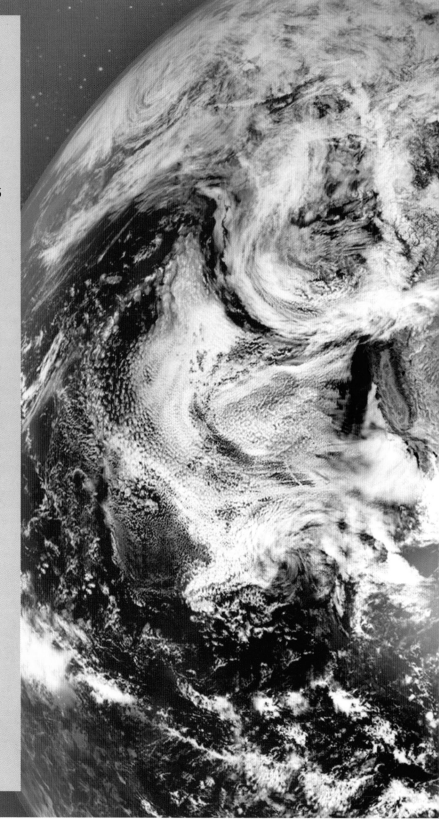

CONTENTS

INTRODUCTION	4
THE BLUE PLANET	8
MOVEMENTS AND COORDINATES	10
THE MOON AND TIDES	12
ECLIPSES	14
THE LONG HISTORY OF THE EARTH	16
STACKED LAYERS	18
THE JOURNEY OF THE PLATES	20
FOLDING IN THE EARTH'S CRUST	22
FLAMING FURNACE	24
DEEP RUPTURE	26
VIOLENT SEAS	28
RISK AREAS	30
GLOBAL EQUILIBRIUM	32
CLIMATE ZONES	34
ATMOSPHERIC DYNAMICS	36
COLLISION	38
LIVING WATER	40
THE LAND AND THE OCEAN	42
THE RAIN ANNOUNCES ITS COMING	44
BRIEF FLASH	48
ANATOMY OF A HURRICANE	50
EVERYTHING CHANGES	52
METAMORPHIC PROCESSES	56
THE BASIS OF LIFE	58
KINGDOMS OF QUIET LIFE	60
AQUATIC PLANTS	62
CONQUEST OF LAND	64
ANATOMY OF A TREE	66
COLORS OF LIFE	68
SEEDS, TO AND FRO	70
POLLINATION	74
ENERGY MANUFACTURERS	76
GLOSSARY	78
INDEX	80

INTRODUCTION

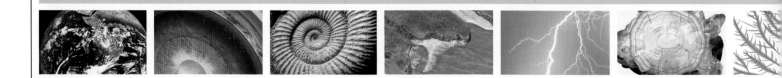

In this book, packed with astounding images and amazing facts, you can explore at leisure our incredible planet, its ancient rocks, violent natural phenomena such as earthquakes and volcanoes, its varied weather and climate, and wonderfully diverse plant life. Fact-filled and lavishly illustrated, here is the story of our world, from its journey around the Sun to the inner secrets of trees and flowers.

Time and Tide

Earth is the only planet in the Solar System where water can exist in its liquid state, and this has enabled the immense variety of life to evolve over billions of years. All the rhythms of life—the seasons, light and darkness, the rise and fall of the oceans—are governed by Earth's ceaseless journey around the Sun and by the circling of our only natural satellite, the Moon. In this book you can discover the effects of the Earth's tilt on its axis, find out how the Moon governs the tides, and how the Earth's magnetism protects our planet from the harmful effects of solar radiation.

Geology and Formation

If the Earth were a plane, rocks would be its "flight recorders." Rocks store information about the past, and geology (the study of rocks) helps scientists reconstruct the long history of the Earth. Rock material originated within the clouds of dust and gases that orbited around the Sun over four billion years ago, and rocks have been silent witnesses to the cataclysms our planet has experienced through the ages. Rock evidence shows how the planet's surface has changed over more than 4 billion years. Even insignificant rocks contain evidence about life millions of years ago.

For ancient civilizations, stones symbolized eternity, but stones endure because their material is recycled time and again. Fifty million years from now, landscapes will not be as we know them—not the Andes, nor the Himalayas, nor the ice of Antarctica, nor the Sahara Desert. Weathering and erosion, slow and relentless, never stop. Yet still there will be rocks, their chemical composition, shape, and texture recording the passage of geological events.

MOUNT KILAUEA
This shield volcano in Hawaii is one of the most active shield volcanoes on Earth.

The forces of nature that shape our planet are unleashed by the movements of rocks deep underground. Earthquakes and volcanoes can unleash rivers of fire, destroy cities, and alter landscapes. Undersea earthquakes can cause tsunamis, waves that spread across the ocean with the speed of an airplane, flooding coastal areas and destroying thousands of lives.

Many ancient civilizations thought of mountain volcanoes as the dwelling places of gods, to explain their awesome fury. Volcanoes spew out lava flows that can change lush landscape into barren wilderness. Hot lava destroys everything in its path, while gas and ash hurled into the air by a volcanic eruption can kill people, animals, and plants. Yet, amazingly, life reemerges, for lava and ash cool and in time make soil unusually fertile.

For this reason many farmers live near "smoking mountains," in spite of the danger. No human can control the forces of nature. All people can do is survive, rebuild, and live again.

Storms and volcanic eruptions are predictable, but not earthquakes, which without warning can spread destruction and death. Throughout its history, Earth has been shaken by earthquakes. Some have done immense damage, such as the earthquake that rocked San Francisco in 1906, registering 8.3 on the Richter scale, and was felt as far away as Oregon to the north. In California, as elsewhere around the world, the earthquake risk remains.

Weather and Climate
"The flutter of a butterfly's wings in Brazil can unleash a tornado in Florida." That was the conclusion in

1972 of Edward Lorenz, an expert in math and meteorology—the study of weather and climate. He was trying to find a way of predicting meteorological phenomena that put people at risk. The Earth's atmosphere is such a complicated system that many scientists define it as chaotic.

No wonder any weather forecast is subject to rapid change. Weather affects people's lives in many ways, and not just when people who planned to go to the beach have to shut themselves up in the basement until a hurricane passes. Wild weather and severe climate disturbance can be catastrophic. People who live in regions subject to tornadoes, hurricanes, or tropical storms, live in fear of disruption and destruction.

Natural phenomena, such as tornadoes, hurricanes, and cyclones, become disasters when they strike populated areas or devastate farmland. Experience shows that we have to learn to live with these events and plan ahead for what might happen when they occur.

In this book you will find useful information about the factors that determine weather and climate, and the methods that are used to make forecasts and predictions. This science helps people plan for and live with adverse weather events, and you will be able to understand why long-term forecasts are so complicated. Such key topics, and more, are all here, to inform and arouse your curiosity about the mighty forces that affect life on Earth.

A World of Plants
There are more than 400,000 plant species in the world, and alongside them live many species of fungi and

SATELLITE IMAGE
In this image of the Earth, you can clearly see the movements of water and air in the atmosphere, causing temperature variations, storms, and droughts.

THE POLLEN REACHES THE STIGMA
This is the first step toward forming a seed. In this magnified image the grains of pollen can be seen on the stigma of wolfsbane (*Arnica montana*).

algae. These organisms flourish and are essential to virtually every environment on Earth, from the frozen tundra of the Arctic region to the lush tropical rainforests.

The first plants on our planet helped to convert bare rock into soil. Here you can discover just how this happened, and what a complex material soil is. There is also an overview of the differences between plants, algae, and fungi.

Without plants, there would be no animal life. Plants made the Earth's atmosphere breathable, and are vital sources of food, medicines, and raw materials. The great forests are precious natural resources, and act as the planet's "lungs." How plants use photosynthesis to convert sunlight into carbohydrates such as sugars and starches is almost magical, as are plants' abilities to adapt to different environments, through adaptations such as moisture-retaining stems, and floating leaves that allow them to live in water. An amazing sequence of images shows how a plant develops from a tiny seed, grows, flowers, and produces seed for the next generation.

Why plants invest so much energy into producing their colorful flowers is another amazing story, and here you can discover how plant fertilization takes place. Did you know that pollination is aided by the wind and insects and that some flowers are pollinated only by one species of insect? Here is a wealth of fascinating information, with spectacular illustrations that take you inside the heart of a tree, to reveal the functions of its tissues down to the tiny veins in its leaves.

The Blue Planet

The Earth is known as the blue planet because of the color of the oceans that cover two thirds of its surface. This planet, the third from the Sun, is the only one we know of where the right conditions exist to sustain life, something that makes the Earth special. It has liquid water in abundance, a mild temperature, and an atmosphere that protects it from solar radiation thanks to its ozone layer. Slightly flattened at its poles and wider at its Equator, the Earth takes 24 hours to revolve once on its axis.

The Phenomenon of Life

Water, in liquid form, makes it possible for life to exist on the Earth. The Earth's average distance from the Sun, along with other factors, means that it is the only planet whose temperatures cover the range from 32°F to 212°F (0°C to 100°C), allowing water to exist as a liquid, and enabling life to develop 3.6 billion years ago.

DISCOVERY FACT™

When seen from space, the planet Earth looks blue because about 70 percent of its surface is covered in water.

-76°F (-60°C)

ONLY ICE
Mars is so far from the Sun that all its water is frozen.

32° to 212°F (0° to 100°C)

THREE STATES
On the Earth, water is found in all three of its possible states.

Above 212°F (100°C)

ONLY STEAM
On Mercury or Venus, which are very close to the Sun, water would evaporate.

1 **EVAPORATION**
Because of the Sun's energy, water enters the atmosphere by evaporating from oceans and, to a lesser extent, from lakes, rivers, and other sources on the continents.

EARTH MOVEMENTS

The Earth moves both in orbit around the Sun and rotating on its own axis.

SUN

93,500,000 miles (150,474,000 km)

ROTATION: The Earth revolves on its axis in 23 hours and 56 minutes.

REVOLUTION: It takes the Earth 365 days, 5 hours, and 57 minutes to travel once around the Sun.

The Moon, our only natural satellite, is four times smaller than the Earth and takes 27.32 days to orbit the Earth.

SOUTH POLE

AXIS
INCLINATION

ROTATION
AXIS

NORTH
POLE

23.5°

This is the inclination of the Earth's axis from the vertical. As the Earth orbits the Sun, different regions gradually receive more or less sunlight, causing the four seasons.

CHARACTERISTICS

CONVENTIONAL
PLANET SYMBOL

⊕

ESSENTIAL DATA

Average distance to the Sun	93 million miles (150 million km)
Revolution around the Sun (Earth year)	365.25 days
Diameter at the Equator	7,926 miles (12,756 km)
Orbiting speed	18.5 miles per second (29.78 km/s)
Mass*	1
Gravity*	1

Density	3.19 ounces per cubic inch (5.52 g/cu cm)
Average temperature	59°F (15°C)

*In both cases, Earth = 1

AXIS INCLINATION

23.5°

One rotation lasts 23.56 hours.

3 PRECIPITATION
The atmosphere loses water through condensation. Gravity causes rain, snow, and hail. Dew and frost directly alter the state of the surface they cover.

2 CONDENSATION
The Earth's winds transport moisture-laden air until weather conditions cause the water vapor to condense into clouds and eventually fall to the ground as rain or other forms of precipitation.

Magnetism and Gravity

The Earth's magnetic field originates in the planet's outer core, where turbulent currents of molten iron generate both electric and magnetic fields. The orientation of the Earth's magnetism varies over time, causing the magnetic poles to fluctuate.

THE EARTH'S
CORE WORKS
AS A MAGNET.

Magnetic force

Solid core

Mantle

The Earth's magnetic field is created by convective currents in its outer core.

The liquid outer core is in constant motion.

WHAT IT DOES
The magnetic field protects the Earth from the radiation of the solar wind.

Some particles are attracted to the poles.

Van Allen belt

Magnetic field lines

Magnetosphere

SOLAR WIND

The Van Allen radiation belts trap the particles from the solar wind, causing phenomena such as the auroras.

Axis

Earth

Magnetic field tail

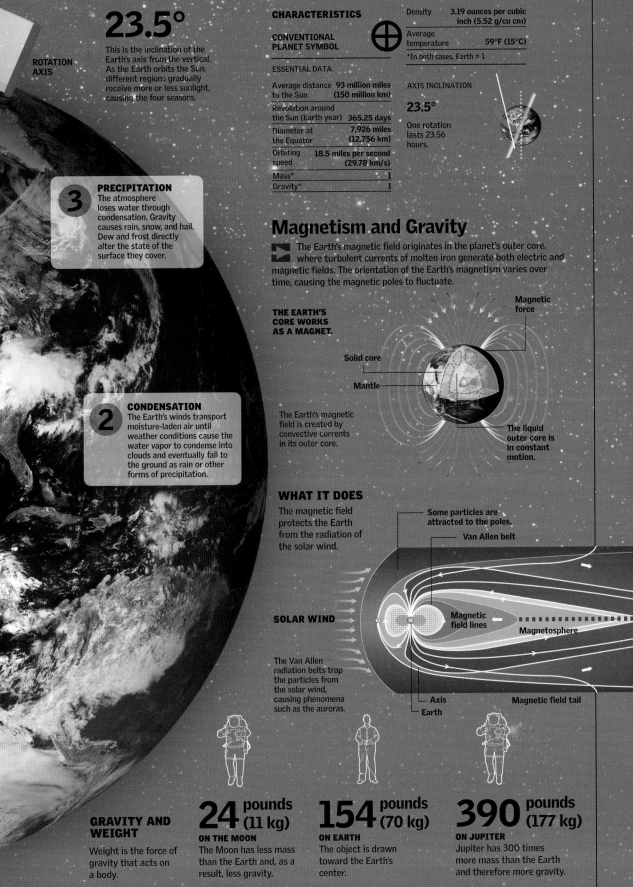

GRAVITY AND WEIGHT

Weight is the force of gravity that acts on a body.

24 pounds (11 kg)
ON THE MOON
The Moon has less mass than the Earth and, as a result, less gravity.

154 pounds (70 kg)
ON EARTH
The object is drawn toward the Earth's center.

390 pounds (177 kg)
ON JUPITER
Jupiter has 300 times more mass than the Earth and therefore more gravity.

Movements and Coordinates

Yes, it moves. The Earth rotates on its axis while simultaneously orbiting the Sun. The natural phenomena of night and day, seasons, and years are caused by these movements. To track the passage of time, calendars, clocks, and time zones were invented. Time zones are divided by the meridians and assigned a reference hour according to their location. When traveling east, an hour is added in each time zone. An hour is subtracted during westbound travel.

The Earth's Movements

Night and day, summer and winter, new year and old year result from the Earth's various movements during its orbit of the Sun. The most important motions are the Earth's daily rotation from west to east on its own axis and its revolution around the Sun. (The Earth follows an elliptical orbit that has the Sun at one of the foci of the ellipse, so the distance to the Sun varies slightly over the course of a year.)

ROTATION
1 DAY
The Earth revolves once on its axis in 23 hours and 56 minutes. We experience this as day and night.

N
23.5°
S

REVOLUTION
1 YEAR
The Earth's orbit around the Sun lasts 365 days, 5 hours, and 57 minutes.

NUTATION
18.6 YEARS
A kind of nod made by the Earth, because of the gravitational pull of the Sun and Moon, causes the displacement of the geographic poles by nine arc seconds.

9°

PRECESSION
25,800 YEARS
A slow turning of the direction of the Earth's axis (similar to that of a top), is caused by the Earth's nonspherical shape and the gravitational forces of the Sun and the Moon.

47°

Equinox and Solstice

Every year, around June 21, the Northern Hemisphere reaches its maximum inclination toward the Sun (a phenomenon referred to as the summer solstice in the Northern Hemisphere and the winter solstice in the Southern Hemisphere). At this time the North Pole receives sunlight all day, while the South Pole is covered in darkness. Between one solstice and another the equinoxes occur, which is when the axis of the Earth points toward the Sun and the periods of daylight and darkness are the same all over the planet.

June 20 or 21

Summer solstice in the Northern Hemisphere and winter solstice in the Southern Hemisphere. Solstices exist because of the tilt of the Earth's axis. The length of the day and the height of the Sun in the sky are greatest in summer and least in winter.

September 21 or 22

Fall equinox in the Northern Hemisphere and spring equinox in the Southern Hemisphere. The Sun passes directly above the Equator, and day and night have the same length.

MEASUREMENT OF TIME
Months and days are charted by calendars and clocks, but the measurement of these units of time is neither a cultural nor an arbitrary construct. Instead, it is derived from the natural movements of the Earth.

March 20 or 21

Spring equinox in the Northern Hemisphere and fall equinox in the Southern Hemisphere. The Sun passes directly above the Equator, and day and night have the same length.

SUN

PERIHELION
The point where the orbiting Earth is nearest the Sun, at a distance of 91.6 million miles (147.5 million km), occurs in January.

23.5°
TILT OF THE EARTH'S AXIS

93
MILLION MILES (150 MILLION KM) AVERAGE DISTANCE FROM THE SUN

December 21 or 22

Winter solstice in the Northern Hemisphere and summer solstice in the Southern Hemisphere. Solstices exist because of the tilt of the Earth's axis. The length of the day and the height of the Sun in the sky are greatest in summer and least in winter.

APHELION
The point in the Earth's orbit where it is farthest from the Sun, at 94 million miles (152 million km), occurs at the beginning of July.

Geographic Coordinates

Thanks to the grid formed by the lines of latitude and longitude, the position of any object on the Earth's surface can be easily located, using the intersection of the Earth's Equator and the Greenwich meridian (longitude 0°), which passes through London, England, as a prime reference point. This intersection marks the midpoint between the Earth's poles.

THE EARTH'S ORBIT
About 365 days

1 day **A DAY**
The period of time it takes the Earth to rotate on its axis.

About 30 days **MONTHS**
The periods of time, between 28 and 31 days, into which a year is divided.

**0°
GREENWICH MERIDIAN**
Northern Hemisphere

PARALLELS

Temperate zone
66.5° N Arctic Circle
23.5° N Tropic of Cancer

Tropical zone
0° EQUATOR

Polar zone
23.5° S Tropic of Capricorn
66.5° S Antarctic Circle

Southern Hemisphere

Time Zones

The Earth is divided into 24 areas, or time zones, each one of which corresponds to an hour assigned according to the Coordinated Universal Time (UTC), using the prime meridian in Greenwich, London, England, as the base meridian. One hour is added when crossing each meridian in an easterly direction, and one hour is subtracted when traveling west.

Jet Lag

The human body's biological clock responds to the rhythms of light and dark created by the passage of night and day. Long air flights east or west interrupt and disorient the body's clock, causing a disorder known as "jet lag." It can cause fatigue, irritability, nausea, headaches, and difficulty sleeping at night.

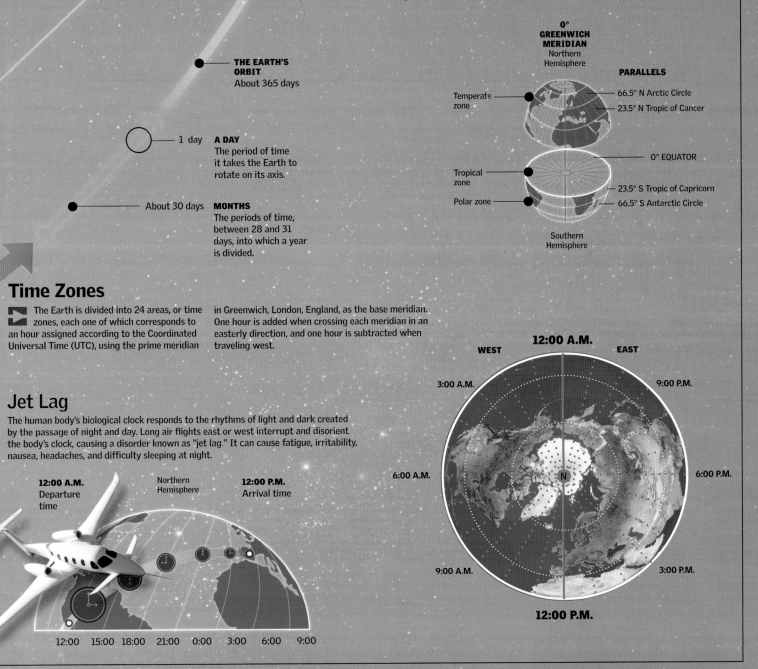

12:00 A.M.
Departure time

Northern Hemisphere

12:00 P.M.
Arrival time

12:00   15:00   18:00   21:00   0:00   3:00   6:00   9:00

12:00 A.M.
WEST   EAST

3:00 A.M.   9:00 P.M.

6:00 A.M.   6:00 P.M.

N

9:00 A.M.   3:00 P.M.

12:00 P.M.

The Moon and Tides

Romance and terror, mystery and superstition—all these emotions are responses to the Moon, the Earth's one natural satellite, which always hides one of its two faces. However, whatever symbolic meanings are attributed to the Moon, its gravitational pull has a concrete effect on the Earth—it is a cause of the tides. Depending on the distance of the Moon from the Earth, the gravitational pull exerted by the Moon varies in strength, and so do high tides and low tides. The effect is greatest on large, open areas of ocean, producing the highest tides, while tides in closed or small bodies of water are much lower.

ORIGIN OF THE MOON
The most widely accepted theory of the Moon's origin suggests that an object the size of Mars collided with the Earth during its formation.

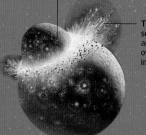

The ejected material scattered into space around the Earth, and over time, it coalesced into the Moon.

ARISTARCHUS
Brightest spot on the Moon.

OCEANUS PROCELLARUM
The largest sea, over 1,800 miles (3,000 km) across.

GRIMALDI

GASSENDI

THE MOON'S MOVEMENTS

As the Moon orbits the Earth, it revolves on its own axis in such a way that it always shows the Earth the same side.

LUNAR MONTH
It takes 29.53 days to complete its phases.

SIDEREAL MONTH
The Moon takes 27.32 days to orbit the Earth.

Hidden face

Visible face

MOON

EARTH

Lunar orbit

HIDDEN FACE
Invisible from the Earth, this side of the Moon was a mystery until 1959, when the Russian probe *Luna 3* managed to photograph the hidden zone. Because of the greater thickness of the Moon's crust on this side, it has fewer seas.

The Tides

The water on the side of the Earth closest to the Moon feels the Moon's gravitational pull most intensely, and vice versa. Two tides are formed, and they track the Moon in its orbit around the Earth. However, they precede the Moon instead of being directly in line with it.

1 NEW MOON
SPRING TIDE
When the Sun and the Moon are aligned, the highest high tides and lowest low tides are produced.

2 FIRST QUARTER
NEAP TIDE
The Moon and the Sun are at right angles to the Earth, producing the lowest high tides and the highest low tides.

3 FULL MOON
SPRING TIDE
The Sun and the Moon align once again, and the Sun augments the Moon's gravitational pull, causing a second spring tide.

4 THIRD QUARTER
NEAP TIDE
The Moon and the Sun again form a right angle, causing a second neap tide.

KEY

Gravitational pull of the Moon

Lunar orbit

Moon

Earth orbit

Gravitational pull of the Sun

Influence on the tide by the gravitational pull of the Moon

Influence on the tide by the gravitational pull of the Sun

Sun

THE SUN'S GRAVITY ALSO INFLUENCES THE TIDES.

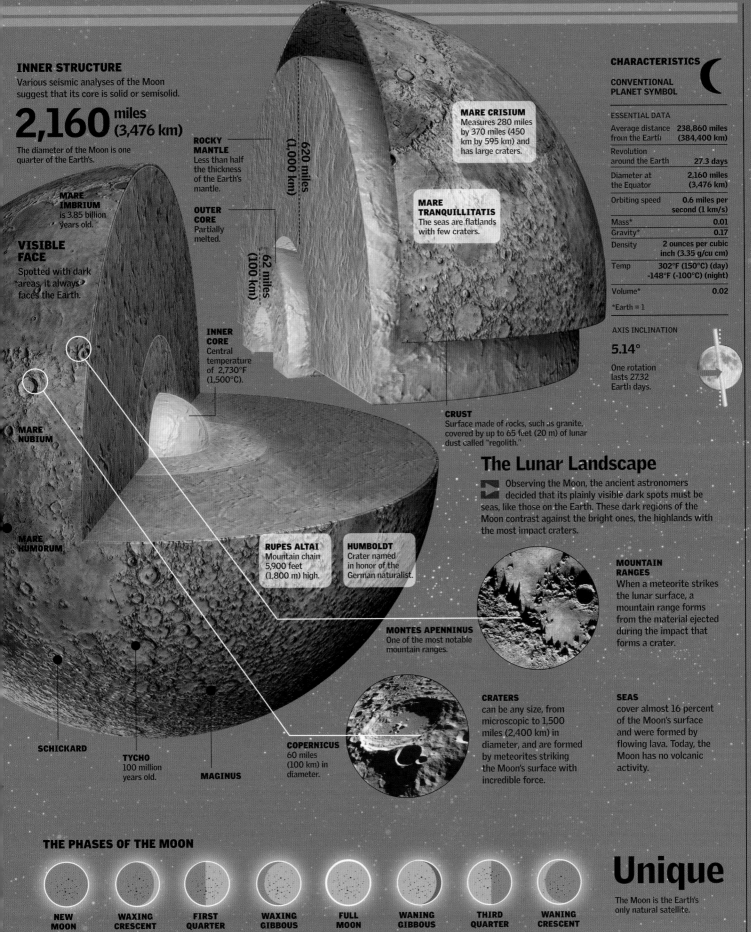

INNER STRUCTURE

Various seismic analyses of the Moon suggest that its core is solid or semisolid.

2,160 miles (3,476 km)

The diameter of the Moon is one quarter of the Earth's.

MARE IMBRIUM is 3.85 billion years old.

VISIBLE FACE

Spotted with dark areas, it always faces the Earth.

MARE NUBIUM

MARE HUMORUM

SCHICKARD

TYCHO 100 million years old.

MAGINUS

ROCKY MANTLE Less than half the thickness of the Earth's mantle.

OUTER CORE Partially melted.

INNER CORE Central temperature of 2,730°F (1,500°C).

620 miles (1,000 km)

62 miles (100 km)

RUPES ALTAI Mountain chain 5,900 feet (1,800 m) high.

HUMBOLDT Crater named in honor of the German naturalist.

MONTES APENNINUS One of the most notable mountain ranges.

COPERNICUS 60 miles (100 km) in diameter.

MARE CRISIUM Measures 280 miles by 370 miles (450 km by 595 km) and has large craters.

MARE TRANQUILLITATIS The seas are flatlands with few craters.

CRUST Surface made of rocks, such as granite, covered by up to 65 feet (20 m) of lunar dust called "regolith."

CHARACTERISTICS

CONVENTIONAL PLANET SYMBOL

ESSENTIAL DATA

Average distance from the Earth	238,860 miles (384,400 km)
Revolution around the Earth	27.3 days
Diameter at the Equator	2,160 miles (3,476 km)
Orbiting speed	0.6 miles per second (1 km/s)
Mass*	0.01
Gravity*	0.17
Density	2 ounces per cubic inch (3.35 g/cu cm)
Temp	302°F (150°C) (day) -148°F (-100°C) (night)
Volume*	0.02

*Earth = 1

AXIS INCLINATION

5.14°

One rotation lasts 27.32 Earth days.

The Lunar Landscape

Observing the Moon, the ancient astronomers decided that its plainly visible dark spots must be seas, like those on the Earth. These dark regions of the Moon contrast against the bright ones, the highlands with the most impact craters.

MOUNTAIN RANGES When a meteorite strikes the lunar surface, a mountain range forms from the material ejected during the impact that forms a crater.

CRATERS can be any size, from microscopic to 1,500 miles (2,400 km) in diameter, and are formed by meteorites striking the Moon's surface with incredible force.

SEAS cover almost 16 percent of the Moon's surface and were formed by flowing lava. Today, the Moon has no volcanic activity.

THE PHASES OF THE MOON

NEW MOON   **WAXING CRESCENT**   **FIRST QUARTER**   **WAXING GIBBOUS**   **FULL MOON**   **WANING GIBBOUS**   **THIRD QUARTER**   **WANING CRESCENT**

Unique

The Moon is the Earth's only natural satellite.

Eclipses

Typically four times a year, during the full or new moon, the centers of the Moon, the Sun, and the Earth become aligned, causing one of the most marvelous celestial phenomena: an eclipse. At these times, the Moon either passes in front of the Sun or passes through the Earth's shadow. The Sun—even during an eclipse—is not safe to look at directly, since it can cause irreparable damage to the eye, burning the retina, so watching this natural wonder requires special high-quality filters or indirect viewing such as projecting the Sun's image through a pinhole onto a sheet of paper. In addition to the spectacle, solar eclipses provide a good opportunity for astronomers to conduct scientific research.

TOTAL LUNAR ECLIPSE, SEEN FROM THE EARTH

The orange color comes from sunlight that has been refracted and colored by the Earth's atmosphere.

ANNULAR ECLIPSE OF THE SUN, SEEN FROM THE EARTH

Solar Eclipse

Solar eclipses occur when the Moon passes directly between the Sun and the Earth, casting a shadow along a path on the Earth's surface. The central cone of the shadow is called the "umbra," and the area of partial shadow around it is called the "penumbra." Viewers in the regions where the umbra falls on the Earth's surface see the Moon's disk completely obscure the Sun—a total solar eclipse. Those watching from the surrounding areas that are located in the penumbra see the Moon's disk cover only part of the Sun—a partial solar eclipse.

ALIGNMENT

Sun   Moon   Earth

During a solar eclipse, astronomers take advantage of the blocked view of the Sun in order to use devices designed to study the Sun's atmosphere.

TYPES OF ECLIPSES

TOTAL
The Moon is between the Sun and the Earth and creates a cone-shaped shadow.

ANNULAR
The Sun appears larger than the Moon, and it remains visible around it.

PARTIAL
The Moon does not cover the Sun completely, so the Sun appears as a crescent.

SUN'S APPARENT SIZE

400
times larger than the Moon

DISCOVERY FACT™

The Moon's apparent size varies because of its elliptical orbit: A total eclipse occurs only if it passes in front of the Sun when near its closest point to Earth.

SUNLIGHT

DISTANCE FROM THE SUN TO THE EARTH

400
times greater than the distance from the Earth to the Moon

Lunar Eclipse

When the Earth passes directly between the full Moon and the Sun, a lunar eclipse (which may be total, partial, or penumbral) occurs. Without the Earth's atmosphere, during each lunar eclipse the Moon would become completely invisible (something that never happens). The totally eclipsed Moon's characteristic reddish color is caused by light refracted by the Earth's atmosphere. During a partial eclipse, on the other hand, part of the Moon falls in the shadow cone, while the rest is in the penumbra, the outermost, palest part. It is not dangerous to look at a lunar eclipse directly.

ALIGNMENT

Sun   Earth   Moon

During an eclipse, the Moon is not completely black but appears reddish.

TYPES OF ECLIPSES

TOTAL
The Moon is completely in the shadow cone.

PARTIAL
The Moon is only partially inside the shadow cone.

PENUMBRAL
The Moon is in the penumbral cone.

Lunar orbit

Shadow cone

NEW MOON
TOTAL ECLIPSE

EARTH

Earth orbit

FULL MOON
TOTAL ECLIPSE

Shadow cone

PARTIAL ECLIPSE

Penumbra cone

PENUMBRAL ECLIPSE

THE ECLIPSE CYCLE

Eclipses repeat every 223 lunations—18 years and 11 days. These are called "Saros periods."

ECLIPSES IN A YEAR

2	7	4
Minimum	Maximum	Average

ECLIPSES IN A SAROS

41	29	70
of the Sun	of the Moon	Total

OBSERVATION FROM EARTH

A black, polymer filter, with an optical density of 5.0, produces a clear orange image of the Sun.

Prevents retinal burns

SOLAR ECLIPSES are different for each local observer.

LUNAR ECLIPSES are the same for all observers.

MAXIMUM DURATION OF SOLAR ECLIPSE
8 minutes

MAXIMUM DURATION OF LUNAR ECLIPSE
100 minutes

ECLIPSES IN 2014 AND BEYOND

OF THE SUN	4/29 Annular	10/23 Partial	3/20 Total	9/13 Partial	3/09 Total	9/01 Annular	2/26 Annular	8/21 Total	2/15 Partial	7/13 Partial	8/11 Partial	1/06 Partial	7/02 Total	12/26 Annular	6/21 Annular	12/14 Annular	6/10 Annular	12/04 Total	4/30 Partial	10/25 Partial	4/20 Hybrid	10/14 Annular

	2014		2015		2016		2017		2018		2019		2020		2021		2022		2023		2024

OF THE MOON	4/15 Total	10/08 Total	4/04 Total	9/28 Total	3/23 Penumbral	9/16 Penumbral	2/11 Partial	8/07 Total	1/31 Total	1/21 Total	7/16 Partial	1/10 6/5 7/5 11/30 Penumbral	5/26 Total	11/19 Partial	5/16 Total	11/08 Total	5/05 Penumbral	10/28 Partial

The Long History of the Earth

The nebular hypothesis developed by astronomers suggests that the Earth was formed in the same way and at the same time as the rest of the planets and the Sun. It all began with an immense cloud of helium and hydrogen and a small portion of heavier materials, 4.6 billion years ago. Earth emerged from one of these "small" revolving clouds, where the particles constantly collided with one another, producing very high temperatures. Later, a series of processes took place that gave the planet its present shape.

From Chaos to Today's Earth

Earth was formed 4.6 billion years ago. In the beginning, it was a body of incandescent rock in the Solar System. The first clear signs of life appeared in the oceans 3.6 billion years ago, and since then life has expanded and diversified. The changes have been unceasing, and, according to experts, there will be many more changes in the future.

4.5
BILLION YEARS AGO

COOLING
The first crust formed as it was exposed to space and cooled. Earth's layers became differentiated by their density.

4.6
BILLION YEARS AGO

FORMATION
The accumulation of matter into solid bodies, a process called "accretion," ended, and the Earth stopped increasing in volume.

60
MILLION YEARS AGO

FOLDING IN THE TERTIARY PERIOD
The folding began that would produce the highest mountains on Earth (the Alps, the Andes, and the Himalayas) and that continues to generate earthquakes even today.

540
MILLION YEARS AGO
PALEOZOIC ERA

FRAGMENTATION
The great landmass Pangaea formed, which would later fragment to provide the origin of the continents that exist today. The oceans reached their greatest rate of expansion.

1.0
BILLION YEARS AGO

SUPERCONTINENTS
Rodinia, the first supercontinent, is believed to have formed, but completely disappeared about 650 million years ago.

4
BILLION YEARS AGO
METEORITE COLLISION

Meteorite collisions, at a rate 150 times as great as that of today, evaporated the primitive ocean and resulted in the rise of all known forms of life.

3.8
BILLION YEARS AGO
ARCHEAN EON
STABILIZATION

The processes that formed the atmosphere, the oceans, and protolife intensified. At the same time, the crust stabilized, and the first plates of Earth's crust appeared. Because of their weight, they sank into Earth's mantle, making way for new plates, a process that continues today.

When the first crust cooled, intense volcanic activity freed gases from the interior of the planet, and those gases formed the atmosphere and the oceans.

THE AGE OF THE SUPER VOLCANOES

Indications of komatiite, an igneous rock that is now found very rarely and only in an altered state.

The oldest rocks appeared.

1.8
BILLION YEARS AGO
PROTEROZOIC EON
CONTINENTS

The first continents, made of light rocks, appeared. In North America (then Laurentia) and in the Baltic, there are large rocky areas that date back to that time.

2.2
BILLION YEARS AGO
WARMING

Earth warmed again, and the glaciers retreated, giving way to the oceans, in which new organisms would be born. The ozone layer began to form.

2.3
BILLION YEARS AGO
"SNOWBALL" EARTH

A hypothetical first, great glaciation.

DISCOVERY FACT™

It is believed that the Moon originated from debris created when another planet, known as Theia, crashed into the Earth while it was still forming.

Stacked Layers

Every 110 feet (33 m) below the Earth's surface, the temperature increases by 1.8 degrees Fahrenheit (1 degree Celsius). To reach the Earth's center—which, in spite of temperatures around 10,800°F (6,000°C), is assumed to be solid because of the enormous pressure exerted on it—a person would have to burrow through four well-defined layers. The gases that cover the Earth's surface are also divided into layers with different compositions. Forces act on the Earth's crust from above and below to sculpt and permanently alter it.

DISCOVERY FACT™

Measured from the Equator, the total distance from the surface to the center of the Earth is 3,965 miles (6,380 km).

Earth's crust

Earth's crust is its solid outer layer, with a thickness of 3–9 miles (5–15 km) under the oceans and up to 44 miles (70 km) under mountain ranges. Volcanoes on land and volcanic activity in the mid-ocean ridges generate new rock, which becomes part of the crust. The rocks at the bottom of the crust tend to melt back into the rocky mantle.

KEY ● Sedimentary Rock ◌ Igneous Rock ◉ Metamorphic Rock

THE CONTINENTAL SHELF
In the area where the oceanic crust comes in contact with a continent, igneous rock is transformed into metamorphic rock by heat and pressure.

THE MID-OCEAN RIDGES
The ocean floor is regenerated with new basaltic rock formed by magma that solidifies in the rifts that run along mid-ocean ridges.

OCEANIC ISLANDS
Some sedimentary rocks are added to the predominantly igneous rock composition.

THE SOLID EXTERIOR
The crust is made up of igneous, sedimentary, and metamorphic rocks, of various typical compositions, according to the terrain.

MOUNTAIN RANGES
Made up of the three types of rocks in roughly equal parts.

GRANITIC BATHOLITHS
Plutons can solidify underground as masses of granite.

PLUTONS
Masses of rising magma that cool within the Earth's crust. Their name is derived from Pluto, the Roman god of the underworld.

INTERNAL ROCK
The inside of a mountain range consists of igneous rock (mostly granite) and metamorphic rock.

COASTAL ROCK
Lithified layers of sediments, usually clay and pebbles, that come from the erosion of high mountains.

CRUST
3–44 miles
(5–70 km)

The Gaseous Envelope

 The air and most of the weather events that affect our lives occur only in the lower layer of the Earth's atmosphere. This relatively thin layer, called the "troposphere," is up to 11 miles (18 km) thick at the Equator but only 5 miles (8 km) thick at the poles. Each layer of the atmosphere has a distinct composition.

Less than
11 miles
(18 km)

TROPOSPHERE
Contains 75 percent of the gas and almost all of the water vapor in the atmosphere.

Less than
30 miles
(50 km)

STRATOSPHERE
Very dry; water vapor freezes and falls out of this layer, which contains the ozone layer.

Less than
50 miles
(80 km)

MESOSPHERE
The temperature is -130°F (-90°C), but it increases gradually above this layer.

Less than
280 miles
(450 km)

THERMOSPHERE
Very low density. Below 155 miles (250 km) it is made up mostly of nitrogen; above that level it is mostly oxygen.

Less than
300 miles
(480 km)

EXOSPHERE
No fixed outer limit. It contains lighter gases such as hydrogen and helium, mostly ionized.

UPPER MANTLE
440 miles
(710 km)

LOWER MANTLE
1,360 miles
(2,200 km)

Composition similar to that of the crust, but in a liquid state and under great pressure, between 1,830° and 8,130°F (1,000° and 4,500°C).

OUTER CORE
1,400 miles
(2,300 km)

Composed mainly of molten iron and nickel among other metals, at temperatures above 8,500°F (4,700°C).

INNER CORE
750 miles
(1,200 km) radius

The inner core behaves as a solid because it is under enormous pressure.

LITHOSPHERE
60 miles
(100 km)

Includes the solid outer part of the upper mantle, as well as the crust.

ASTHENOSPHERE
300 miles
(480 km)

Underneath is the asthenosphere, made up of partially molten rock.

The Journey of the Plates

When geophysicist Alfred Wegener suggested in 1910 that the continents were moving, the idea seemed fantastic. There was no way to explain the idea. Only a half-century later, plate tectonic theory was able to offer an explanation of the phenomenon. Volcanic activity on the ocean floor, convection currents, and the melting of rock in the mantle power the continental drift that is still molding the planet's surface today.

Continental Drift

The first ideas on continental drift proposed that the continents floated on the ocean. That idea proved inaccurate. The seven tectonic plates contain portions of ocean beds and continents. They drift on the molten mantle like sections of a giant shell. Depending on the direction in which they move, their boundaries can converge (when they tend to come together), diverge (when they tend to separate), or slide horizontally past each other (along a transform fault).

The Hidden Motor

Convection currents in the molten rock propel the crust. Rising magma forms new sections of crust at divergent boundaries. At convergent boundaries, the crust melts into the mantle. Thus, the tectonic plates act like a conveyor belt on which the continents travel.

250 MILLION YEARS AGO

The landmass from which today's continents come was a single block (Pangaea) surrounded by the ocean.

PANGAEA

...180 MILLION YEARS AGO

The North American Plate has separated, as has the Antarctic Plate. The supercontinent Gondwana (South America and Africa) has started to divide and form the South Atlantic. India is separating from Africa.

LAURASIA

GONDWANA

ANTARCTICA

2 inches (5 cm)

Typical distance the plates travel in a year.

CONVERGENT BOUNDARY
When two plates collide, one sinks below the other, forming a subduction zone. This causes folding in the crust and volcanic activity.

INDO-AUSTRALIAN PLATE

TONGA TRENCH

NAZCA PLATE

EASTERN PACIFIC RIDGE

PERU-CHILE TRENCH

CONVECTION CURRENTS
The hottest molten rock rises; once it has risen, it cools and sinks again. This process causes continuous currents in the mantle.

OUTWARD MOVEMENT
The action of the magma causes the tectonic plate to move toward a subduction zone at its far end.

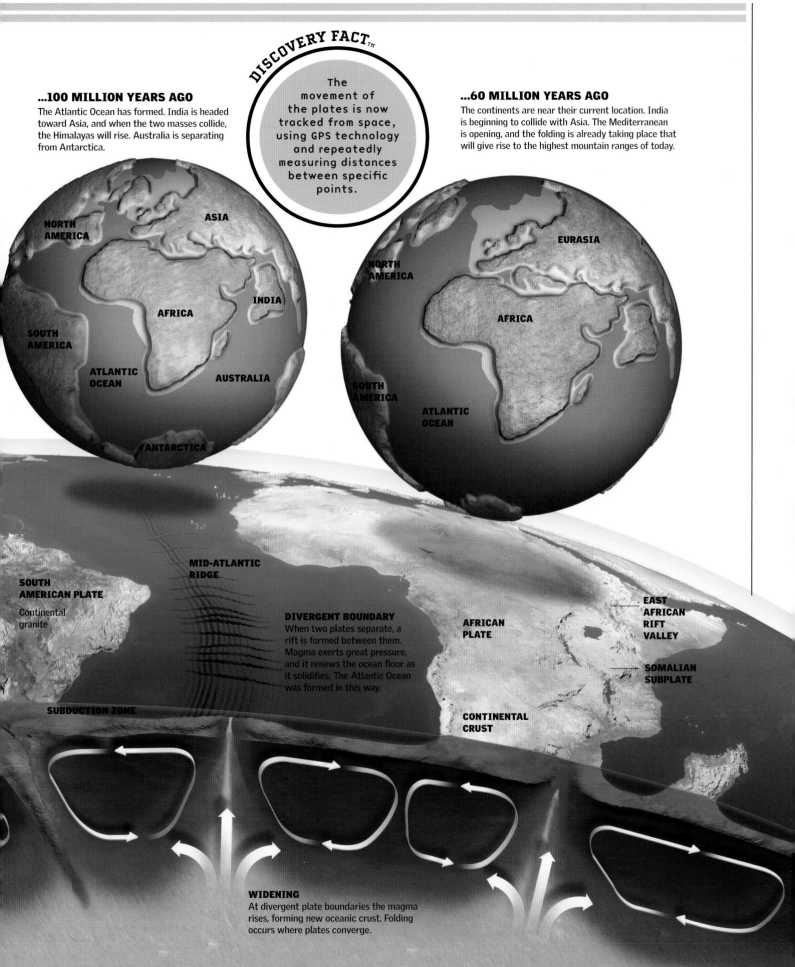

...100 MILLION YEARS AGO

The Atlantic Ocean has formed. India is headed toward Asia, and when the two masses collide, the Himalayas will rise. Australia is separating from Antarctica.

DISCOVERY FACT™

The movement of the plates is now tracked from space, using GPS technology and repeatedly measuring distances between specific points.

...60 MILLION YEARS AGO

The continents are near their current location. India is beginning to collide with Asia. The Mediterranean is opening, and the folding is already taking place that will give rise to the highest mountain ranges of today.

NORTH AMERICA
ASIA
AFRICA
INDIA
SOUTH AMERICA
ATLANTIC OCEAN
AUSTRALIA
ANTARCTICA

NORTH AMERICA
EURASIA
AFRICA
SOUTH AMERICA
ATLANTIC OCEAN

SOUTH AMERICAN PLATE
Continental granite

MID-ATLANTIC RIDGE

DIVERGENT BOUNDARY
When two plates separate, a rift is formed between them. Magma exerts great pressure, and it renews the ocean floor as it solidifies. The Atlantic Ocean was formed in this way.

AFRICAN PLATE

EAST AFRICAN RIFT VALLEY

SOMALIAN SUBPLATE

CONTINENTAL CRUST

SUBDUCTION ZONE

WIDENING
At divergent plate boundaries the magma rises, forming new oceanic crust. Folding occurs where plates converge.

Folding in the Earth's Crust

The movement of tectonic plates causes distortions and breaks in the Earth's crust, especially in convergent plate boundaries. Over millions of years, these distortions produce larger features called "folds," which become mountain ranges. Certain characteristic types of terrain give clues about the great folding processes in Earth's geological history.

Distortions of the Crust

The crust is composed of layers of solid rock. Tectonic forces, resulting from the differences in speed and direction between plates, make these layers stretch like elastic, flow, or break. Mountains are formed in processes requiring millions of years. Then external forces, such as erosion from wind, ice, and water, come into play. If slippage releases rock from the pressure that is deforming it elastically, the rock tends to return to its former state and can cause earthquakes.

1 A portion of the crust subjected to a sustained horizontal tectonic force is met by resistance, and the rock layers become deformed.

2 The outer rock layers, which are often more rigid, fracture and form a fault. If one rock boundary slips underneath another, a thrust fault is formed.

3 The composition of rock layers shows the origin of the folding, despite the effects of erosion.

The Three Greatest Folding Events

The Earth's geological history has included three major mountain-building processes, called "orogenies." The mountains created during the first two orogenies (the Caledonian and the Hercynian) are much lower today because they have undergone millions of years of erosion.

MATERIALS
Mostly granite, slate, amphibolite, gneiss, quartzite, and schist.

Brachiopods

MATERIALS
Mudstone, slate, and sandstone, in lithified layers.

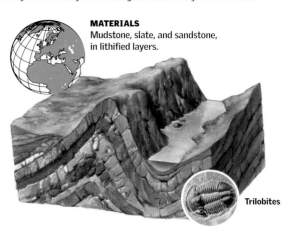

Trilobites

430 Million Years

CALEDONIAN OROGENY
Formed the Caledonian range. Remnants can be seen in Scotland, the Scandinavian Peninsula, and Canada (which all collided at that time).

300 Million Years

HERCYNIAN OROGENY
Took place between the late Devonian and the early Permian Periods. It was more important than the Caledonian Orogeny. It shaped central and western Europe and produced large veins of iron ore and coal. This orogeny gave rise to the Ural Mountains, the Appalachian range in North America, part of the Andes, and Tasmania.

Formation of the Himalayas

The highest mountains on Earth were formed following the collision of India and Eurasia. The Asian landmass bent and the plate doubled in thickness, forming the Tibetan plateau. The Indian Plate is still sliding horizontally underneath the Asiatic Plate. A sedimentary block trapped between the plates is cutting the upper part of the Asiatic Plate into segments that are piling on top of each other. This deeply fractured section of the old plate is called an "accretionary prism." The folding process gave rise to the Himalayan range, which includes the highest mountain on the planet, Mount Everest (29,029 feet [8,848 m]).

SOUTHEAST ASIA

INDIA TODAY

10 MILLION YEARS AGO

20 MILLION YEARS AGO

30 MILLION YEARS AGO

Ammonites

MATERIALS
High proportions of sediment in Nepal, batholiths in the Asiatic Plate, and intrusions of new granite: iron, tin, and tungsten.

60 MILLION YEARS

ALPINE OROGENY
Began in the Cenozoic Era and continues today. This orogeny raised the entire system of mountain ranges that includes the Pyrenees, the Alps, the Caucasus, and even the Himalayas. It also gave the American Rockies and the Andes Mountains their current shape.

A COLLISION OF CONTINENTS

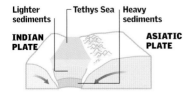

Lighter sediments — Tethys Sea — Heavy sediments

INDIAN PLATE — **ASIATIC PLATE**

60 MILLION YEARS AGO
The Tethys Sea gives way as the plates approach. Layers of sediment begin to rise.

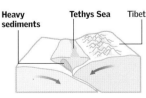

Heavy sediments — Tethys Sea — Tibet

40 MILLION YEARS AGO
As the two plates approach each other, a subduction zone begins to form.

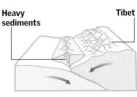

Heavy sediments — Tibet

20 MILLION YEARS AGO
The Tibetan plateau is pushed up by pressure from settling layers of sediment.

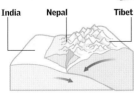

India — Nepal — Tibet

THE HIMALAYAS TODAY
The movement of the plates continues to fold the crust, and the land of Nepal is slowly disappearing.

Flaming Furnace

Volcanoes are among the most powerful manifestations of our planet's dynamic interior. The magma they release at the Earth's surface can cause phenomena that devastate surrounding areas: explosions, enormous flows of molten rock, fire and ash that rain from the sky, floods, and mudslides. Every volcano has a life cycle, during which it can modify the topography and the climate and after which it becomes extinct.

DISCOVERY FACT™

Since ancient times, human beings have feared volcanoes, even seeing their smoking craters as entrances to the underworld.

Life and Death of a Volcano: the Formation of a Caldera

1 Explosive eruptions can expel huge quantities of lava, gas, and rock.

2 A void is left in the conduit and in the internal chamber.

MOUNTAIN-RANGE VOLCANOES

Many volcanoes are caused by phenomena occurring in subduction zones along convergent plate boundaries.

1 When two plates converge, one moves under the other (subduction).

2 The rock melts and forms new magma. Great pressure builds up between the plates.

3 The heat and pressure in the crust force the magma to seep through cracks in the rock and rise to the surface, causing volcanic eruptions.

CRATER
Depression or hollow from which eruptions expel magmatic materials (lava, gas, steam, ash, etc.)

PARASITIC VOLCANO
Composite volcanic cones have more than one crater.

SECONDARY CONDUIT

ERUPTION OF LAVA

CLOUD OF ASH

STREAMS OF LAVA
flow down the flanks of the volcano.

VOLCANIC CONE
Made of layers of igneous rock, formed from previous eruptions. Each lava flow adds a new layer.

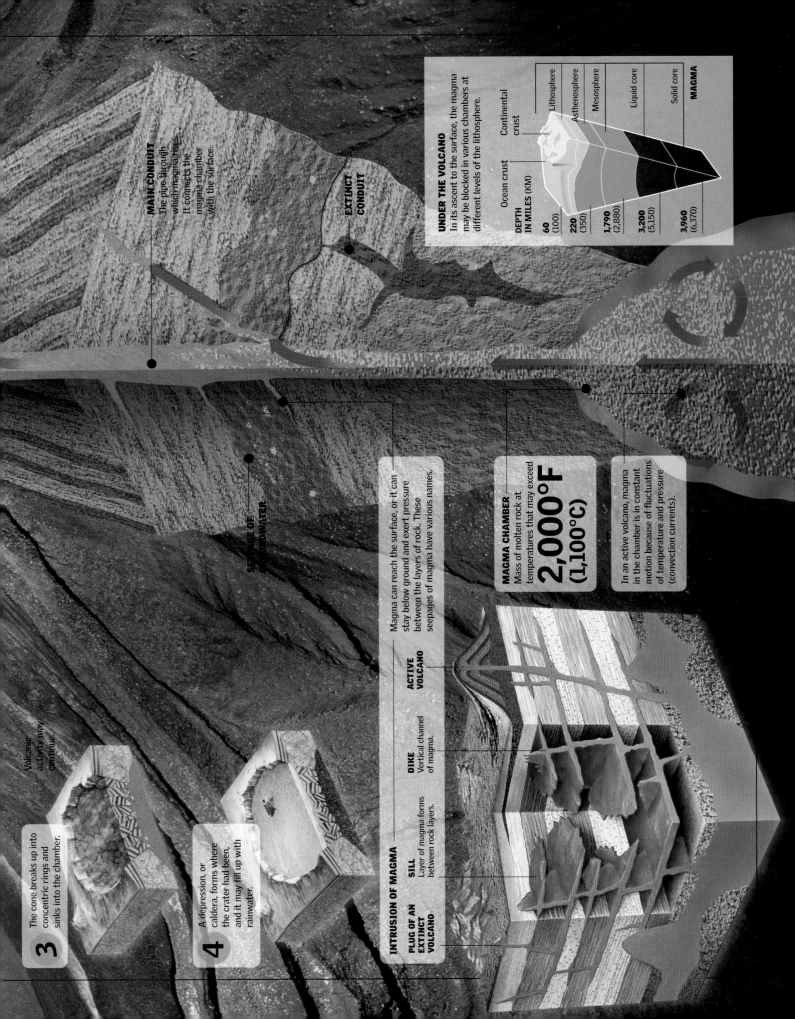

MAIN CONDUIT
The pipe through which magma rises. It connects the magma chamber with the surface.

EXTINCT CONDUIT

UNDER THE VOLCANO
In its ascent to the surface, the magma may be blocked in various chambers at different levels of the lithosphere.

DEPTH IN MILES (KM)	
60 (100)	Lithosphere — Continental crust / Ocean crust
220 (350)	Asthenosphere
1,790 (2,880)	Mesosphere
3,200 (5,150)	Liquid core
3,960 (6,370)	Solid core

MAGMA

SEEPAGE OF GROUNDWATER

Magma can reach the surface, or it can stay below ground and exert pressure between the layers of rock. These seepages of magma have various names.

INTRUSION OF MAGMA

DIKE
Vertical channel of magma.

SILL
Layer of magma forms between rock layers.

PLUG OF AN EXTINCT VOLCANO

ACTIVE VOLCANO

MAGMA CHAMBER
Mass of molten rock at temperatures that may exceed

2,000°F (1,100°C)

In an active volcano, magma in the chamber is in constant motion because of fluctuations of temperature and pressure (convection currents).

3 The cone breaks up into concentric rings and sinks into the chamber.

Volcanic activity may continue.

4 A depression, or caldera, forms where the crater had been, and it may fill up with rainwater.

Deep Rupture

E arthquakes take place because tectonic plates are in constant motion, and therefore they collide with, slide past, and, in some cases, even slip on top of each other. The Earth's crust does not give outward signs of all the movement within it. Instead, energy builds up from these movements within its rocks until the tension is more than the rock can bear. At this point the energy is released at the weakest parts of the crust. This causes the ground to move suddenly, unleashing an earthquake.

1 **FORESHOCK**
A small tremor that can anticipate an earthquake by days or even years. It could be strong enough to move a parked car.

2 **AFTERSHOCK**
New seismic movement that can take place after an earthquake. At times it can be even more destructive than the earthquake itself.

EARTHQUAKES PER YEAR

MAGNITUDE	QUANTITY
8 or Greater	1
7 to 7.9	18
6 to 6.9	120
5 to 5.9	800
4 to 4.9	6,200
3 to 3.9	49,000

EPICENTER
Point on the Earth's surface located directly above the focus.

HYPOCENTER OR FOCUS
Point of rupture, where the disturbance originates. Can be up to 435 miles (700 km) below the surface.

ALPINE FAULT

7.05

7.65 RICHTER

30 seconds
The time lapse between each tremor of the Earth's crust.

PLAIN

FOLDS
These result from tension that accumulates between tectonic plates. Earthquakes release part of the tension energy generated by orogenic folds.

Origin of an Earthquake

1

TENSION IS GENERATED
The plates move in opposite directions, sliding along the fault line. At a certain point along the fault, they catch on each other. Tension begins to increase between the plates.

2

TENSION VERSUS RESISTANCE
Because the force of displacement is still active even when the plates are not moving, the tension grows. Rock layers near the boundary are distorted and crack.

3

EARTHQUAKE
When the rock's resistance is overcome, it breaks and suddenly shifts, causing an earthquake typical of a transform-fault boundary.

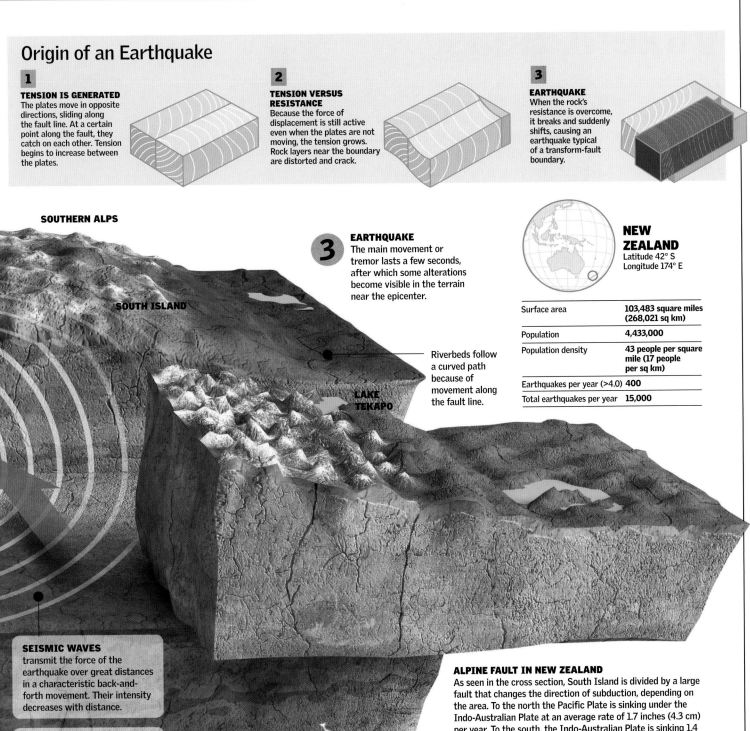

SOUTHERN ALPS

SOUTH ISLAND

3 **EARTHQUAKE**
The main movement or tremor lasts a few seconds, after which some alterations become visible in the terrain near the epicenter.

Riverbeds follow a curved path because of movement along the fault line.

LAKE TEKAPO

NEW ZEALAND
Latitude 42° S
Longitude 174° E

Surface area	103,483 square miles (268,021 sq km)
Population	4,433,000
Population density	43 people per square mile (17 people per sq km)
Earthquakes per year (>4.0)	400
Total earthquakes per year	15,000

SEISMIC WAVES
transmit the force of the earthquake over great distances in a characteristic back-and-forth movement. Their intensity decreases with distance.

FAULT PLANE
Usually curves rather than following a straight line. This irregularity causes the tectonic plates to collide, which leads to earthquakes as the plates move.

ALPINE FAULT IN NEW ZEALAND
As seen in the cross section, South Island is divided by a large fault that changes the direction of subduction, depending on the area. To the north the Pacific Plate is sinking under the Indo-Australian Plate at an average rate of 1.7 inches (4.3 cm) per year. To the south, the Indo-Australian Plate is sinking 1.4 inches (3.6 cm) per year under the Pacific Plate.

FUTURE DEFORMATION OF THE ISLAND

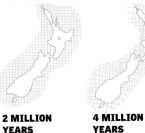

To the west there is a plain that has traveled nearly 310 miles (500 km) to the north in the past 20 million years.

2 MILLION YEARS

4 MILLION YEARS

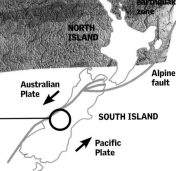

NORTH ISLAND

Potential earthquake zone

Alpine fault

Australian Plate

SOUTH ISLAND

Pacific Plate

15 miles (25 km)
Average depth of the Earth's crust below the island.

Violent Seas

A large earthquake or volcanic eruption can cause a tsunami, which means "wave in the harbor" in Japanese. Tsunamis travel very fast, up to 500 miles per hour (800 km/h). On reaching shallow water, they decrease in speed but increase in height. A tsunami can become a wall of water up to 100 feet (30 m) high on approaching the shore. The height depends partly on the shape of the beach and the depth of coastal waters. If the wave reaches dry land, it can inundate vast areas and cause considerable damage. A 1960 earthquake off the coast of Chile caused a tsunami that swept away communities along 500 miles (800 km) of the coast of South America. Twenty-two hours later the waves reached the coast of Japan, where they damaged coastal towns.

The word **tsunami** comes from Japanese

TSU NAMI
Harbor   Wave

How It Happens

A tremor that generates vibrations on the ocean surface can be caused by seismic movement on the seafloor. Most of the time the tremor is caused by the upward or downward movement of a block of oceanic crust that moves a mass of ocean water. A volcanic eruption, meteorite impact, or nuclear explosion can also cause a tsunami.

90%
Movement of tectonic plates

10%
Other causes

RISING PLATE

Water level rises   Water level drops

SINKING PLATE

The displaced water tends to level out, generating the force that causes waves.

7.5

Only earthquakes above this magnitude on the Richter scale can produce a tsunami strong enough to cause damage.

THE EARTHQUAKE
A movement of the ocean floor displaces an enormous mass of water upward.

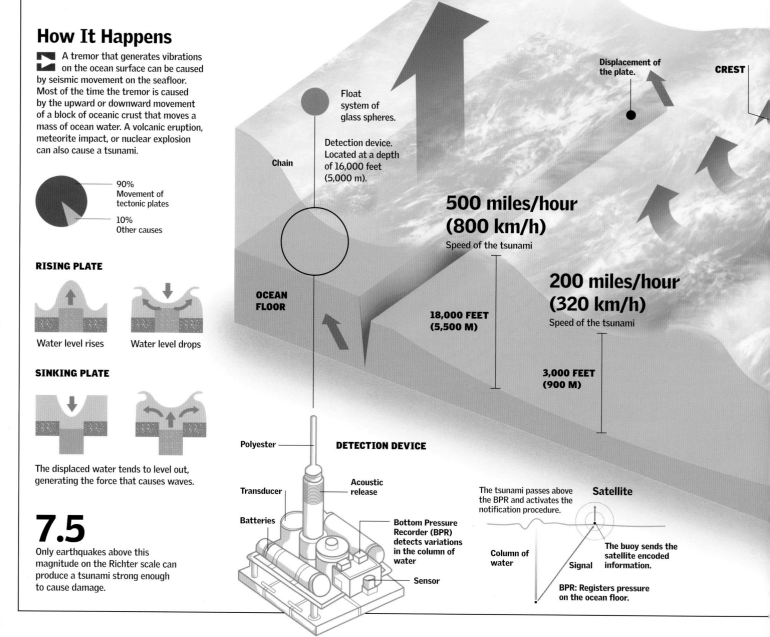

Displacement of the plate.

CREST

Float system of glass spheres.

Detection device. Located at a depth of 16,000 feet (5,000 m).

Chain

500 miles/hour (800 km/h)
Speed of the tsunami

200 miles/hour (320 km/h)
Speed of the tsunami

OCEAN FLOOR

18,000 FEET (5,500 M)

3,000 FEET (900 M)

Polyester

DETECTION DEVICE

Transducer

Batteries

Acoustic release

Bottom Pressure Recorder (BPR) detects variations in the column of water

Sensor

The tsunami passes above the BPR and activates the notification procedure.

Satellite

Column of water

Signal

The buoy sends the satellite encoded information.

BPR: Registers pressure on the ocean floor.

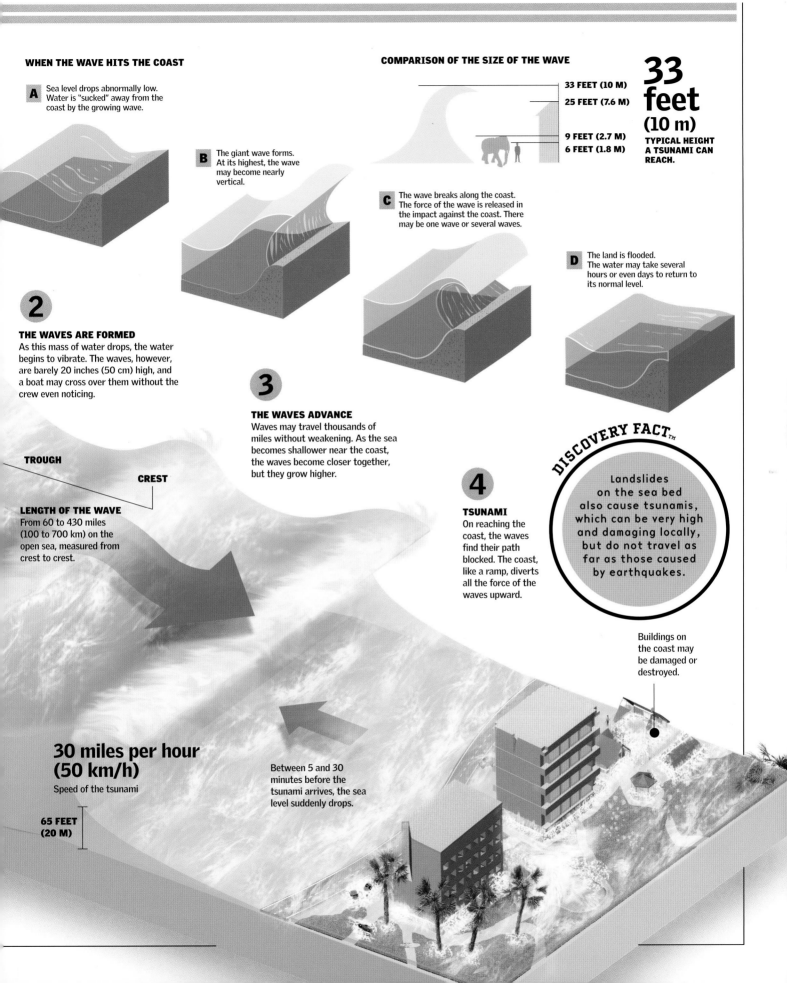

WHEN THE WAVE HITS THE COAST

A Sea level drops abnormally low. Water is "sucked" away from the coast by the growing wave.

B The giant wave forms. At its highest, the wave may become nearly vertical.

C The wave breaks along the coast. The force of the wave is released in the impact against the coast. There may be one wave or several waves.

D The land is flooded. The water may take several hours or even days to return to its normal level.

COMPARISON OF THE SIZE OF THE WAVE

33 FEET (10 M)
25 FEET (7.6 M)
9 FEET (2.7 M)
6 FEET (1.8 M)

33 feet (10 m)
TYPICAL HEIGHT A TSUNAMI CAN REACH.

2

THE WAVES ARE FORMED
As this mass of water drops, the water begins to vibrate. The waves, however, are barely 20 inches (50 cm) high, and a boat may cross over them without the crew even noticing.

TROUGH

CREST

LENGTH OF THE WAVE
From 60 to 430 miles (100 to 700 km) on the open sea, measured from crest to crest.

3

THE WAVES ADVANCE
Waves may travel thousands of miles without weakening. As the sea becomes shallower near the coast, the waves become closer together, but they grow higher.

4

TSUNAMI
On reaching the coast, the waves find their path blocked. The coast, like a ramp, diverts all the force of the waves upward.

DISCOVERY FACT™
Landslides on the sea bed also cause tsunamis, which can be very high and damaging locally, but do not travel as far as those caused by earthquakes.

Buildings on the coast may be damaged or destroyed.

30 miles per hour (50 km/h)
Speed of the tsunami

Between 5 and 30 minutes before the tsunami arrives, the sea level suddenly drops.

65 FEET (20 M)

Risk Areas

A seismic area is found wherever there is an active fault, and these faults are very numerous throughout the world. The fractures are especially common near mountain ranges and mid-ocean ridges. Unfortunately, many population centers were built up in regions near these dangerous places, and, when an earthquake occurs, they become disaster areas. Where the tectonic plates collide, the risk is even greater.

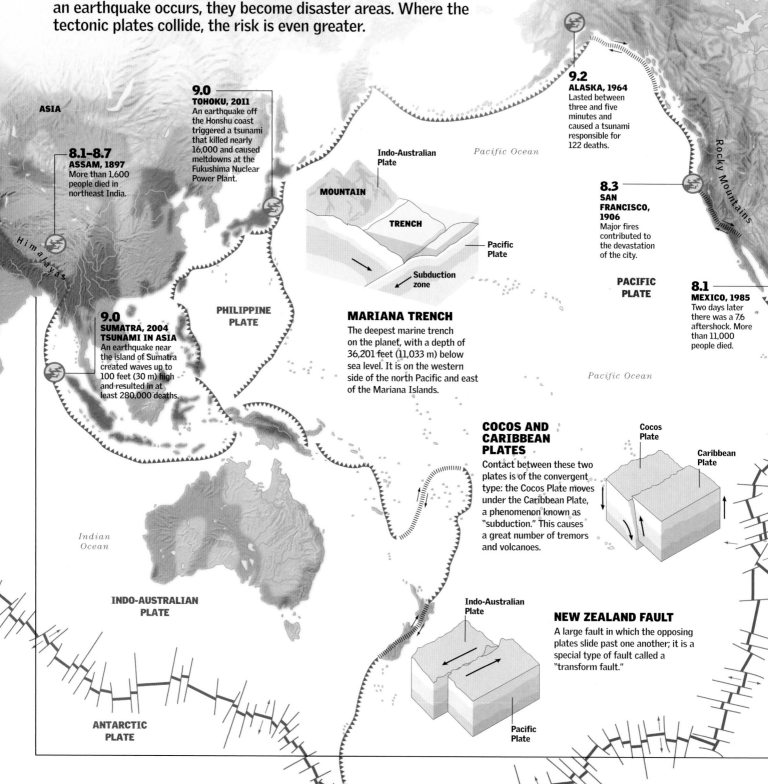

Arctic Ocean

ASIA

8.1–8.7
ASSAM, 1897
More than 1,600 people died in northeast India.

Himalayas

9.0
TOHOKU, 2011
An earthquake off the Honshu coast triggered a tsunami that killed nearly 16,000 and caused meltdowns at the Fukushima Nuclear Power Plant.

9.0
SUMATRA, 2004 TSUNAMI IN ASIA
An earthquake near the island of Sumatra created waves up to 100 feet (30 m) high and resulted in at least 280,000 deaths.

PHILIPPINE PLATE

Indo-Australian Plate

Pacific Ocean

MOUNTAIN

TRENCH

Pacific Plate

Subduction zone

MARIANA TRENCH
The deepest marine trench on the planet, with a depth of 36,201 feet (11,033 m) below sea level. It is on the western side of the north Pacific and east of the Mariana Islands.

9.2
ALASKA, 1964
Lasted between three and five minutes and caused a tsunami responsible for 122 deaths.

Rocky Mountains

8.3
SAN FRANCISCO, 1906
Major fires contributed to the devastation of the city.

PACIFIC PLATE

8.1
MEXICO, 1985
Two days later there was a 7.6 aftershock. More than 11,000 people died.

Pacific Ocean

COCOS AND CARIBBEAN PLATES
Contact between these two plates is of the convergent type: the Cocos Plate moves under the Caribbean Plate, a phenomenon known as "subduction." This causes a great number of tremors and volcanoes.

Cocos Plate

Caribbean Plate

Indian Ocean

INDO-AUSTRALIAN PLATE

Indo-Australian Plate

NEW ZEALAND FAULT
A large fault in which the opposing plates slide past one another; it is a special type of fault called a "transform fault."

Pacific Plate

ANTARCTIC PLATE

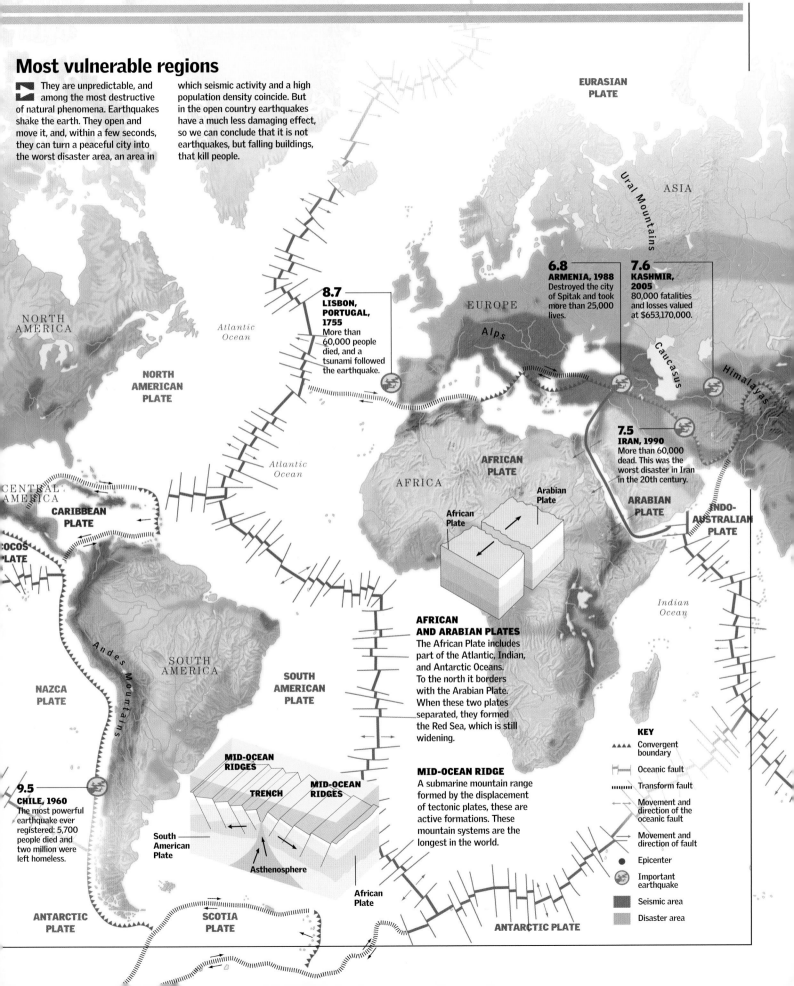

Most vulnerable regions

They are unpredictable, and among the most destructive of natural phenomena. Earthquakes shake the earth. They open and move it, and, within a few seconds, they can turn a peaceful city into the worst disaster area, an area in which seismic activity and a high population density coincide. But in the open country earthquakes have a much less damaging effect, so we can conclude that it is not earthquakes, but falling buildings, that kill people.

EURASIAN PLATE

Ural Mountains

ASIA

EUROPE

Alps

6.8
ARMENIA, 1988
Destroyed the city of Spitak and took more than 25,000 lives.

7.6
KASHMIR, 2005
80,000 fatalities and losses valued at $653,170,000.

Caucasus

Himalayas

8.7
LISBON, PORTUGAL, 1755
More than 60,000 people died, and a tsunami followed the earthquake.

Atlantic Ocean

NORTH AMERICA

NORTH AMERICAN PLATE

Atlantic Ocean

CENTRAL AMERICA

CARIBBEAN PLATE

COCOS PLATE

AFRICA

AFRICAN PLATE

7.5
IRAN, 1990
More than 60,000 dead. This was the worst disaster in Iran in the 20th century.

ARABIAN PLATE

Arabian Plate

African Plate

INDO-AUSTRALIAN PLATE

Indian Ocean

AFRICAN AND ARABIAN PLATES
The African Plate includes part of the Atlantic, Indian, and Antarctic Oceans. To the north it borders with the Arabian Plate. When these two plates separated, they formed the Red Sea, which is still widening.

NAZCA PLATE

Andes Mountains

SOUTH AMERICA

SOUTH AMERICAN PLATE

MID-OCEAN RIDGES

TRENCH

MID-OCEAN RIDGES

South American Plate

Asthenosphere

African Plate

MID-OCEAN RIDGE
A submarine mountain range formed by the displacement of tectonic plates, these are active formations. These mountain systems are the longest in the world.

9.5
CHILE, 1960
The most powerful earthquake ever registered: 5,700 people died and two million were left homeless.

ANTARCTIC PLATE

SCOTIA PLATE

ANTARCTIC PLATE

KEY
▲▲▲▲ Convergent boundary
Oceanic fault
Transform fault
Movement and direction of the oceanic fault
Movement and direction of fault
● Epicenter
Important earthquake
Seismic area
Disaster area

Global Equilibrium

The Sun's radiation delivers a large amount of energy to the Earth, which propels the extraordinary mechanism called the "climatic system." The components of this complex system are the atmosphere, hydrosphere, lithosphere, cryosphere, and biosphere. All these components are constantly interacting with one another via an interchange of materials and energy. The weather and climatic phenomena that have shaped our world in the past, and that we experience today, are the combined expression of Earth's climatic system.

WINDS
The atmosphere is always in motion. Heat displaces masses of air, and this leads to the general circulation of the atmosphere.

Atmosphere

Part of the energy received from the Sun is captured by the atmosphere. The other part is absorbed by the Earth or reflected in the form of heat. Greenhouse gases heat up the atmosphere by slowing the release of heat to space.

Biosphere

Living beings (such as plants) influence weather and climate. They form the foundations of ecosystems, which use minerals, water, and other chemical compounds. They contribute materials to other subsystems.

PRECIPITATION
Water condensing in the atmosphere forms droplets, and gravitational action causes them to fall to the Earth's surface as rain, hail, or snow.

EVAPORATION
Evaporation from the surface of bodies of water maintains the quantity of water vapor in the atmosphere within normal limits.

5–15%
ALBEDO OF THE TROPICAL FORESTS

HEAT

NIGHT AND DAY, COASTAL BREEZES EXCHANGE ENERGY BETWEEN THE HYDROSPHERE AND THE LITHOSPHERE.

MARINE CURRENTS

Hydrosphere

The hydrosphere is the name for all water in liquid form that is part of the climatic system. Most of the lithosphere is covered by liquid water, and some water also circulates through it.

7–10%
ALBEDO OF THE OCEANS

Sun

Essential for climatic activity. About 50 percent of the solar energy reaches the surface of the Earth; some is transferred directly to different layers of the atmosphere and some escapes to outer space. The subsystems absorb, exchange, and reflect energy that reaches the Earth's surface. For example, the biosphere incorporates solar energy via photosynthesis and intensifies the activity of the hydrosphere.

SUN

Cryosphere

Represents regions of the Earth covered by ice. Permafrost exists where the temperature of the soil or rocks is below zero. These regions reflect almost all the light they receive and play a role in the circulation of the ocean, regulating its temperature and salinity.

80% ALBEDO OF RECENTLY FALLEN SNOW

Lithosphere

This is the uppermost solid layer of the Earth's surface. Its continual formation and destruction change the surface of the Earth and can have a large impact on weather and climate. For example, a mountain range may act as a physical barrier to wind and moisture.

50% ALBEDO OF LIGHT CLOUDS

HEAT

HUMAN ACTIVITY

SMOKE
Minute particles of dust and ash that escape into the atmosphere act as condensation nuclei for water vapor.

RETURN TO THE SEA

UNDERGROUND CIRCULATION
The circulation of water is produced by gravity. Water from the hydrosphere infiltrates the lithosphere and circulates there until it reaches the large water reservoirs of lakes, rivers, and oceans.

ASHES
Volcanic eruptions bring nutrients to the climatic system, where the ashes fertilize the soil. Eruptions also block the rays of the Sun and thus reduce the amount of solar radiation received by the Earth's surface. This causes cooling of the atmosphere.

GREENHOUSE EFFECT
Some gases in the atmosphere are very effective at retaining heat. The layer of air near the Earth's surface acts as a shield that establishes a range of temperatures on it, within which life can exist.

SOLAR ENERGY

ATMOSPHERE

STRATOSPHERE

TROPOSPHERE

OZONE LAYER

Climate Zones

Different places in the world, even if far removed from each other, can be grouped into climate zones—that is, into regions that are homogeneous in terms of climatic elements, such as temperature, pressure, rain, and humidity. There is some disagreement among climatologists about the number and description of these regions, but the illustrations given on this map are generally accepted.

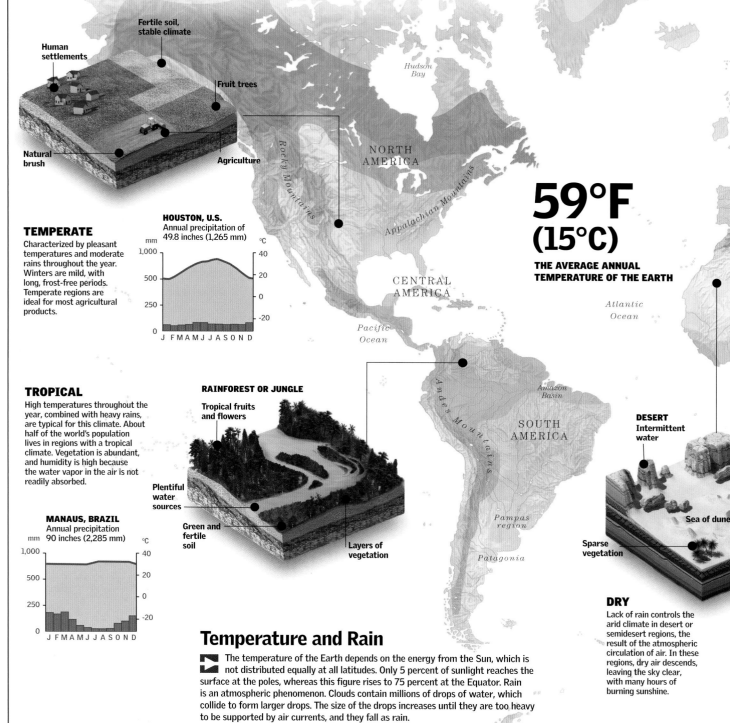

Ice cap

Human settlements

Fertile soil, stable climate

Fruit trees

Natural brush

Agriculture

Rocky Mountains

Hudson Bay

NORTH AMERICA

Appalachian Mountains

TEMPERATE

Characterized by pleasant temperatures and moderate rains throughout the year. Winters are mild, with long, frost-free periods. Temperate regions are ideal for most agricultural products.

HOUSTON, U.S.
Annual precipitation of 49.8 inches (1,265 mm)

mm
1,000
500
250
0
J F M A M J J A S O N D

°C
40
20
0
-20

CENTRAL AMERICA

Pacific Ocean

Atlantic Ocean

59°F (15°C)

THE AVERAGE ANNUAL TEMPERATURE OF THE EARTH

TROPICAL

High temperatures throughout the year, combined with heavy rains, are typical for this climate. About half of the world's population lives in regions with a tropical climate. Vegetation is abundant, and humidity is high because the water vapor in the air is not readily absorbed.

RAINFOREST OR JUNGLE

Tropical fruits and flowers

Plentiful water sources

Green and fertile soil

Layers of vegetation

Andes Mountains

Amazon Basin

SOUTH AMERICA

Pampas region

Patagonia

DESERT
Intermittent water

Sea of dunes

Sparse vegetation

MANAUS, BRAZIL
Annual precipitation 90 inches (2,285 mm)

mm
1,000
500
250
0
J F M A M J J A S O N D

°C
40
20
0
-20

Temperature and Rain

The temperature of the Earth depends on the energy from the Sun, which is not distributed equally at all latitudes. Only 5 percent of sunlight reaches the surface at the poles, whereas this figure rises to 75 percent at the Equator. Rain is an atmospheric phenomenon. Clouds contain millions of drops of water, which collide to form larger drops. The size of the drops increases until they are too heavy to be supported by air currents, and they fall as rain.

DRY

Lack of rain controls the arid climate in desert or semidesert regions, the result of the atmospheric circulation of air. In these regions, dry air descends, leaving the sky clear, with many hours of burning sunshine.

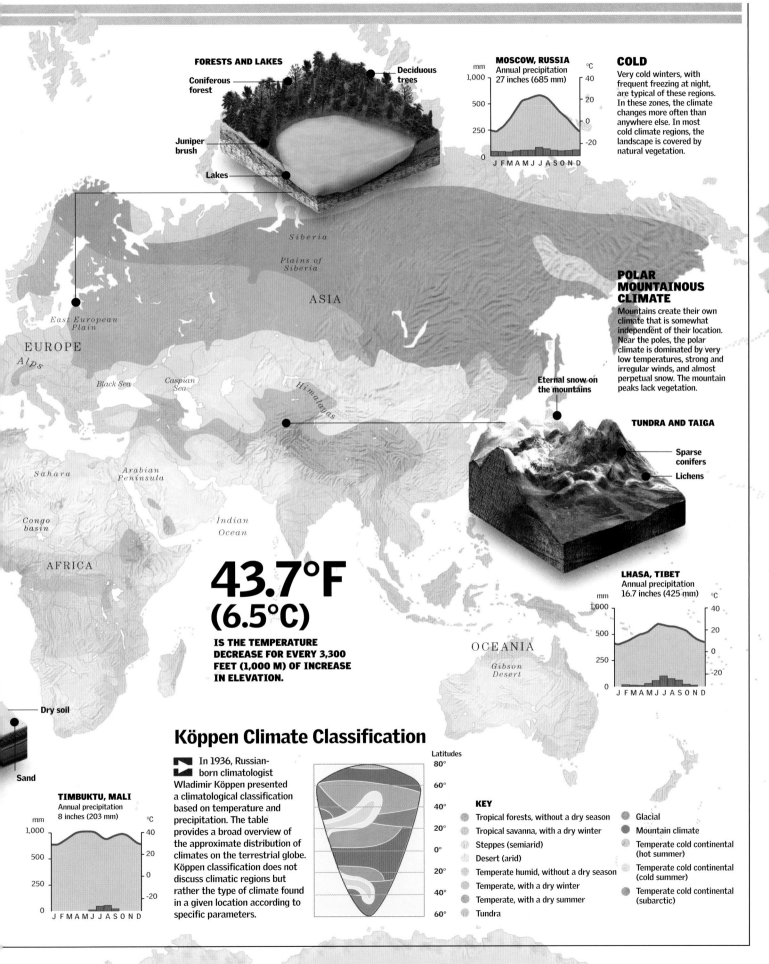

FORESTS AND LAKES

Coniferous forest

Deciduous trees

Juniper brush

Lakes

MOSCOW, RUSSIA
Annual precipitation
27 inches (685 mm)

mm
1,000
500
250
0

°C
40
20
0
-20

J F M A M J J A S O N D

COLD

Very cold winters, with frequent freezing at night, are typical of these regions. In these zones, the climate changes more often than anywhere else. In most cold climate regions, the landscape is covered by natural vegetation.

Siberia

Plains of Siberia

ASIA

EUROPE

Alps

East European Plain

Black Sea

Caspian Sea

Himalayas

POLAR MOUNTAINOUS CLIMATE

Mountains create their own climate that is somewhat independent of their location. Near the poles, the polar climate is dominated by very low temperatures, strong and irregular winds, and almost perpetual snow. The mountain peaks lack vegetation.

Eternal snow on the mountains

TUNDRA AND TAIGA

Sparse conifers

Lichens

Sahara

Arabian Peninsula

Congo basin

Indian Ocean

AFRICA

OCEANIA

Gibson Desert

LHASA, TIBET
Annual precipitation
16.7 inches (425 mm)

mm
1,000
500
250
0

°C
40
20
0
-20

J F M A M J J A S O N D

43.7°F (6.5°C)

IS THE TEMPERATURE DECREASE FOR EVERY 3,300 FEET (1,000 M) OF INCREASE IN ELEVATION.

Dry soil

Sand

TIMBUKTU, MALI
Annual precipitation
8 inches (203 mm)

mm
1,000
500
250
0

°C
40
20
0
-20

J F M A M J J A S O N D

Köppen Climate Classification

In 1936, Russian-born climatologist Wladimir Köppen presented a climatological classification based on temperature and precipitation. The table provides a broad overview of the approximate distribution of climates on the terrestrial globe. Köppen classification does not discuss climatic regions but rather the type of climate found in a given location according to specific parameters.

Latitudes
80°
60°
40°
20°
0°
20°
40°
60°

KEY

- Tropical forests, without a dry season
- Tropical savanna, with a dry winter
- Steppes (semiarid)
- Desert (arid)
- Temperate humid, without a dry season
- Temperate, with a dry winter
- Temperate, with a dry summer
- Tundra

- Glacial
- Mountain climate
- Temperate cold continental (hot summer)
- Temperate cold continental (cold summer)
- Temperate cold continental (subarctic)

Atmospheric Dynamics

The atmosphere is a dynamic system. Temperature changes and the Earth's motion are responsible for horizontal and vertical air displacement. The air of the atmosphere circulates between the poles and the Equator in horizontal bands within different latitudes. In addition, the characteristics of the Earth's surface alter the path of the moving air, causing zones of differing air densities. The interactions between these processes influence the climatic conditions of our planet.

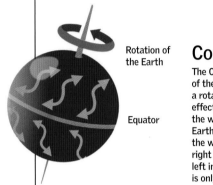

Rotation of the Earth

Equator

Coriolis Force

The Coriolis effect is an apparent deflection of the path of an object that moves within a rotating coordinate system. The Coriolis effect appears to deflect the trajectory of the winds that move over the surface of the Earth, because the Earth is moving beneath the winds. This apparent deflection is to the right in the Northern Hemisphere and to the left in the Southern Hemisphere. The effect is only noticeable on a large scale because of the rotational velocity of the Earth.

FERREL CELL
Between the Hadley and Polar cells, in latitudes of 30–60°, air moves in the opposite direction and is also influenced by the jet stream.

INTERTROPICAL CONVERGENCE ZONE
Near the Equator the Trade Winds converge, giving rise to flat calms (the "Doldrums") and violent storms.

TRADE WINDS
These winds blow toward the Equator from the northeast and southeast.

- Low-pressure area
+ High-pressure area

High and Low Pressure

Warm air rises and causes a low-pressure area (cyclone) to form beneath it. As the air cools and descends, it forms a high-pressure area (anticyclone). At the surface the air moves from an anticyclonic toward a cyclonic area as wind. The warm air, as it is displaced and forced upward, leads to the formation of clouds.

1
Masses of cold air descend and prevent clouds from forming.

6
The masses of cold air lose their mobility.

3
The wind blows from a high- toward a low-pressure area.

5
The rising air leads to the formation of clouds.

A

B

2
The descending air forms an area of high pressure (anticyclone).

4
Warm air rises and forms an area of low pressure (cyclone).

Jet-stream currents

Changes in Circulation

Irregularities in the topography of the surface, abrupt changes in temperature, and the influence of ocean currents can alter the general circulation of the atmosphere. These circumstances can generate waves in the air currents that are, in general, linked to the cyclonic zones. It is in these zones that storms originate, and they are therefore studied with great interest. However, the anticyclone and the cyclone systems must be studied together because cyclones are fed by currents of air coming from anticyclones.

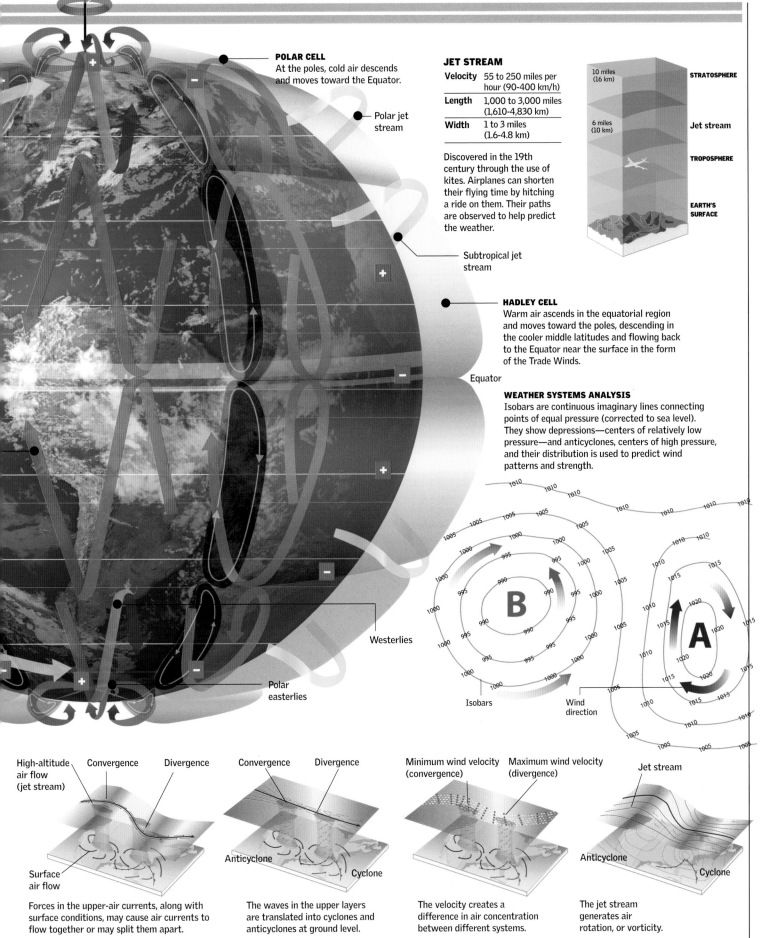

POLAR CELL
At the poles, cold air descends and moves toward the Equator.

Polar jet stream

JET STREAM

Velocity	55 to 250 miles per hour (90-400 km/h)
Length	1,000 to 3,000 miles (1,610-4,830 km)
Width	1 to 3 miles (1.6-4.8 km)

Discovered in the 19th century through the use of kites. Airplanes can shorten their flying time by hitching a ride on them. Their paths are observed to help predict the weather.

10 miles (16 km)   **STRATOSPHERE**

6 miles (10 km)   **Jet stream**

TROPOSPHERE

EARTH'S SURFACE

Subtropical jet stream

HADLEY CELL
Warm air ascends in the equatorial region and moves toward the poles, descending in the cooler middle latitudes and flowing back to the Equator near the surface in the form of the Trade Winds.

Equator

WEATHER SYSTEMS ANALYSIS
Isobars are continuous imaginary lines connecting points of equal pressure (corrected to sea level). They show depressions—centers of relatively low pressure—and anticyclones, centers of high pressure, and their distribution is used to predict wind patterns and strength.

Westerlies

Polar easterlies

Isobars

Wind direction

High-altitude air flow (jet stream)   Convergence   Divergence

Surface air flow

Forces in the upper-air currents, along with surface conditions, may cause air currents to flow together or may split them apart.

Convergence   Divergence

Anticyclone

Cyclone

The waves in the upper layers are translated into cyclones and anticyclones at ground level.

Minimum wind velocity (convergence)   Maximum wind velocity (divergence)

The velocity creates a difference in air concentration between different systems.

Jet stream

Anticyclone

Cyclone

The jet stream generates air rotation, or vorticity.

Collision

When two air masses with different temperatures and moisture content collide, they cause atmospheric disturbances. When the warm air rises, its cooling causes water vapor to condense, forming clouds and precipitation. A mass of warm and light air is always forced upward, while the colder and heavier air acts like a wedge. This cold-air wedge undercuts the warmer air mass and forces it to rise more rapidly. This effect can cause variable, sometimes stormy, weather.

Cold Fronts

These fronts occur when cold air is moved by the wind and collides with warmer air. The warm air is driven upward. The water vapor contained in it forms cumulus clouds, which are rising, dense white clouds. Cold fronts can cause the temperature to drop by 10°–30°F (about 5°–15°C) and are characterized by violent and irregular winds. Their collision with the mass of ascending water vapor will generate rain, snow flurries, and snow. If the condensation is rapid, heavy downpours, snowstorms (during the cold months), and hail may result. On weather maps, the symbol for a cold front is a blue line of triangles indicating the direction of motion.

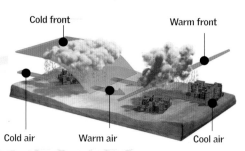

Very dense clouds that rise to a considerable altitude

Cold front

Warm front

Cold air

Warm air

Cool air

Severe imbalance in the cold front

The cold front forces the warm air upward, causing storms.

Behind the cold front, the sky clears and the temperature drops.

There could be precipitation in the area with warm weather.

Rossby Waves

These long horizontal atmospheric waves are associated with the polar-front jet stream, and appear as large undulations in the path of the jet stream. The dynamics of the climatic system are affected by these waves because they promote the exchange of energy between low and high latitudes and can even cause cyclones to form.

1 A long Rossby wave develops in the jet stream of the high troposphere.

2 The Coriolis effect accentuates the wave action in the polar air current.

3 The formation of a meander of warm and cold air can provide the conditions needed to generate cyclones.

Entire Continents

Fronts stretch over large geographic areas. In the example shown on the right, a cold front is causing storm perturbations in western Europe, while to the east, a warm front, extending over a wide area of Poland, brings light rain. These fronts can gain or lose force as they move over the Earth's surface, depending on the global pressure system.

GERMANY
BELARUS
POLAND
Kiev
Bonn *Prague*
Kraków
UKRAINE
FRANCE

KEY
Surface cold front   Surface warm front

STATIONARY FRONTS

These fronts occur when there is no forward motion of warm or cold air—that is, both masses of air are stationary. This type of condition can last many days and produces only altocumulus clouds. The temperature also remains stable, and there is no wind except for some flow of air parallel to the line of the front. There could be some light precipitation.

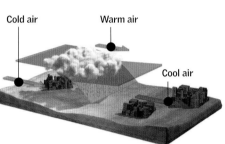

Cold air   Warm air

Cool air

125 miles (200 km)

A WARM FRONT CAN BE 125 MILES (200 KM) LONG. A COLD FRONT USUALLY COVERS ABOUT 60 MILES (100 KM). IN BOTH CASES, THE ALTITUDE IS ROUGHLY 0.6 MILE (1 KM).

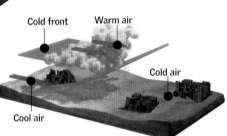

Cold front   Warm air

Cold air

Cool air

OCCLUDED FRONTS

When the cold air replaces the cool air at the surface, with a warm air mass above, a cold occlusion is formed. A warm occlusion occurs when the cool air rises above the cold air. These fronts are associated with rain or snow, cumulus clouds, slight temperature fluctuations, and light winds.

Warm Fronts

These are formed by the action of winds. A mass of warm air occupies a place formerly occupied by a mass of cold air. The speed of the cold air mass, which is heavier, decreases at ground level by friction, through contact with the ground. The warm front ascends and slides above the cold mass. Light rain, snow, or sleet are typically produced, with relatively light winds. The first indications of warm fronts are cirrus clouds, some 600 miles (1,000 km) in front of the advancing low pressure center. Next, layers of stratified clouds, such as the cirrostratus, altostratus, and nimbostratus, are formed while the pressure is decreasing.

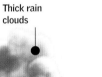

Thick rain clouds

Rain below the front

A barely noticeable imbalance of a warm front

As the clouds extend over a region, they produce light rain or snow.

The mass of cold air takes the form of a retreating wedge, which has the effect of lifting the warm air as it moves over the mass of cold air.

If the warm front moves faster than the retreating wedge of cold air, the height of the advancing warm front continues to increase.

Living Water

The water in the oceans, rivers, clouds, and rain is in constant motion. Surface water evaporates, water in the clouds precipitates, and this precipitation runs along and seeps into the Earth. Nonetheless, the total amount of water on the planet does not change. The circulation and conservation of water is driven by the hydrologic, or water, cycle. This cycle begins with evaporation of water from the Earth's surface. The water vapor humidifies as the air rises. The water vapor in the air cools and condenses onto solid particles as microdroplets. The microdroplets combine to form clouds. When the droplets become large enough, they begin to fall back to Earth, and, depending on the temperature of the atmosphere, they return to the ground as rain, snow, or hail.

1 EVAPORATION
Through the effects of the Sun, ocean water is warmed and fills the air with water vapor. Evaporation from humid soil and vegetation increases humidity. The result is the formation of clouds.

GASEOUS STATE
The rays of the Sun increase the motion of atmospheric gases. The combination of heat and wind transforms liquid water into water vapor.

All the molecules of water are freed.

TRANSPIRATION
Perspiration is a natural process that regulates body temperature. When the body temperature rises, the sweat glands are stimulated, causing perspiration.

CONTRIBUTION OF LIVING BEINGS, ESPECIALLY PLANTS,
10% TO THE WATER IN THE ATMOSPHERE

THE HUMAN BODY IS 65% WATER.

3 The water vapor escapes via micropores in the leaves' surface.

2 The water ascends via the stem.

1 The root absorbs water.

Root cells

2 CONDENSATION
In order for water vapor to condense and form clouds, the air must contain particles to act as condensation nuclei, allowing the molecules of water to form microdroplets. For condensation to occur, the water must be cooled.

FORMATION OF DROPLETS
The molecules of water vapor decrease their mobility and begin to collect on solid particles suspended in the air.

Nucleus

CLOUDS

OCEAN

RIVER

DISCHARGE AREA

6 RETURN TO THE OCEAN
The waters return to the ocean, completing the cycle, which can take days for surface waters and years for underground waters.

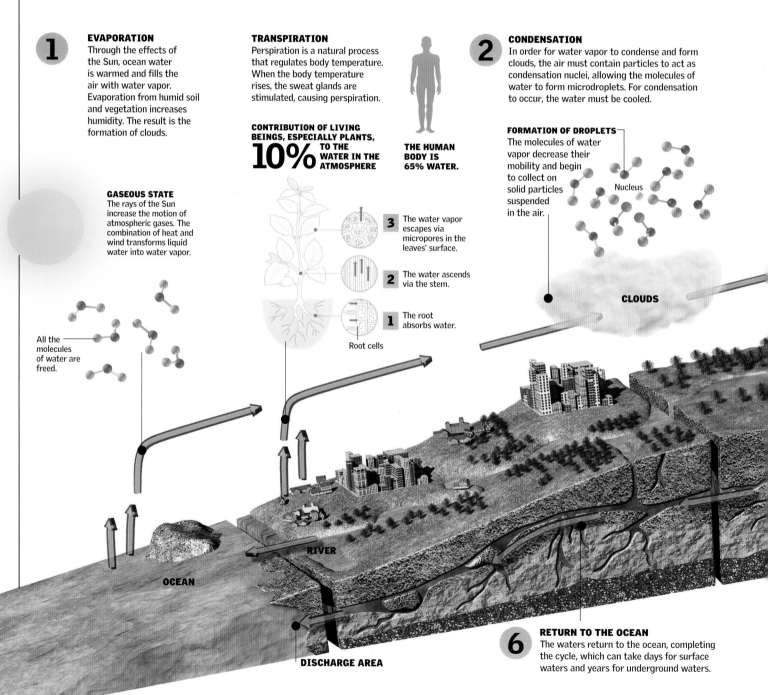

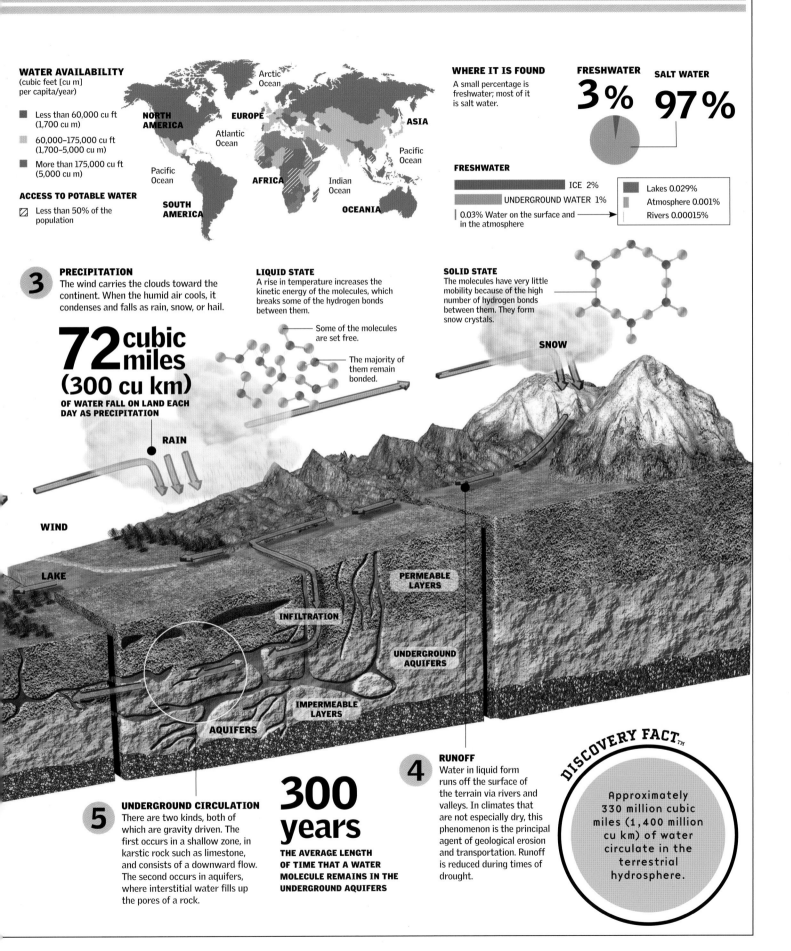

WATER AVAILABILITY
(cubic feet [cu m]
per capita/year)

- Less than 60,000 cu ft
  (1,700 cu m)
- 60,000–175,000 cu ft
  (1,700–5,000 cu m)
- More than 175,000 cu ft
  (5,000 cu m)

ACCESS TO POTABLE WATER

- Less than 50% of the
  population

WHERE IT IS FOUND
A small percentage is
freshwater; most of it
is salt water.

FRESHWATER
3%

SALT WATER
97%

FRESHWATER

ICE 2%
UNDERGROUND WATER 1%
0.03% Water on the surface and
in the atmosphere

Lakes 0.029%
Atmosphere 0.001%
Rivers 0.00015%

3 **PRECIPITATION**
The wind carries the clouds toward the
continent. When the humid air cools, it
condenses and falls as rain, snow, or hail.

LIQUID STATE
A rise in temperature increases the
kinetic energy of the molecules, which
breaks some of the hydrogen bonds
between them.

Some of the molecules
are set free.

The majority of
them remain
bonded.

SOLID STATE
The molecules have very little
mobility because of the high
number of hydrogen bonds
between them. They form
snow crystals.

SNOW

72 cubic miles
(300 cu km)
**OF WATER FALL ON LAND EACH
DAY AS PRECIPITATION**

RAIN

WIND

LAKE

**PERMEABLE
LAYERS**

INFILTRATION

**UNDERGROUND
AQUIFERS**

**IMPERMEABLE
LAYERS**

AQUIFERS

5 **UNDERGROUND CIRCULATION**
There are two kinds, both of
which are gravity driven. The
first occurs in a shallow zone, in
karstic rock such as limestone,
and consists of a downward flow.
The second occurs in aquifers,
where interstitial water fills up
the pores of a rock.

300
years
**THE AVERAGE LENGTH
OF TIME THAT A WATER
MOLECULE REMAINS IN THE
UNDERGROUND AQUIFERS**

4 **RUNOFF**
Water in liquid form
runs off the surface of
the terrain via rivers and
valleys. In climates that
are not especially dry, this
phenomenon is the principal
agent of geological erosion
and transportation. Runoff
is reduced during times of
drought.

DISCOVERY FACT™

Approximately
330 million cubic
miles (1,400 million
cu km) of water
circulate in the
terrestrial
hydrosphere.

The Land and the Ocean

Temperature distribution and, above all, temperature differences very much depend on the proximity of different regions to large bodies of water. Water absorbs heat and releases it more slowly than the land does, which is why a body of water can moderate the temperature of the environment around it. Its influence is unmistakable in coastal areas. In addition, this difference between the land and the sea is the cause of coastal winds. In clear weather, the land heats up during the day, which causes the air to rise rapidly and form a low-pressure zone, which draws in marine breezes.

MOUNTAIN WINDS

CHINOOK WINDS

The winds that blow down the leeward side of a mountain range are dry and warm, sometimes quite hot, occurring in various places of the world. In the western United States, they are called "chinooks" and are capable of making snow disappear within minutes.

Humid winds are lifted over the slopes, creating clouds and precipitation on the windward side. These are called "anabatic" winds.

The dry "katabatic" wind blows down the mountain slope on the leeward side, warming as it descends.

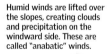

LEEWARD

WINDWARD

Winds	Characteristics	Location
Autan	Dry and mild	Southwestern France
Berg	Dry and warm	South Africa
Bora	Dry and cold	Northeastern Italy
Brickfielder	Dry and hot	Australia
Buran	Dry and cold	Mongolia
Harmattan	Dry and cool	North Africa
Levant	Humid and mild	Mediterranean region
Mistral	Dry and cold	Rhône Valley, France
Santa Ana	Dry and hot	Southern California
Sirocco	Dry and hot	Southern Europe and North Africa
Tramontana	Dry and cold	Northeast Spain
Zonda	Dry and mild	Western Argentina

WINDS OF THE MOUNTAINS AND VALLEYS

1 The Sun heats the soil of the valley and the surrounding air, which ascends by convection.

2 The air is cooled as it ascends, becomes more dense, and descends. Then it heats up again and repeats the cycle.

VALLEY

SLOPE

80%
RECENT SNOW

75%
THICK CLOUDS

15%
ALBEDO OF MEADOWS

ABSORPTION OF HEAT

DAY

1 Cold air currents descend from the mountainside toward the floor of the valley, which is still hot.

2 The air currents are heated and ascend by convection. When they rise, they cool and once again descend along the mountainside.

MOUNTAINSIDE

VALLEY

NIGHT

RELEASE OF HEAT

WARM AIR WHIRLWINDS

Intense heat on the plains can generate a hot, spiral-formed column of air sometimes more than 300 feet (100 m) high.

1 Strong, high-speed winds move on top of weaker winds and cause the intermediate air to be displaced like a pencil on a table.

2 A powerful air current lifts the spiral.

STRONG WIND

MILD WIND

HEAT ISLANDS

Cities are complex surfaces. Concrete and asphalt absorb a large quantity of heat during sunny days and release it during the night. Factories and vehicles emit large amounts of heat into the atmosphere.

ISOTHERMS IN A TYPICAL CITY (° F)

81   81
82   82
84   84
84   84
82   82

84   86   88   90   86   82
   82   90   88   84

CONTINENTALITY

In the interior of a landmass, there is a wide variation of daily temperatures, while on the coasts, the influence of the ocean reduces this variation. This continentality effect is very noticeable in the United States, Russia, India, and Australia.

CONTINENTALITY INDEX

Less   More

DAILY VARIATION OF TEMPERATURES IN THE UNITED STATES

+ ALBEDO → – ENERGY ABSORBED

25% WET SAND

3–5% WATER (WHEN THE SUN IS HIGH)

50% LIGHT CLOUDS

5–15% FORESTS

Forests absorb a significant amount of heat but remain cool because much energy is used to evaporate the moisture.

COASTAL BREEZES

1 **ON THE LAND**
During the day, the land heats up more rapidly than the ocean. The warm air rises and is replaced by cooler air coming from the sea.

WARM AIR
LAND

Because it is opaque, the heat stays in the surface layers, which are heated and cooled rapidly.

IN THE OCEAN
From the coast, the ocean receives air that loses its heat near the water. As a result, the colder air descends toward the sea.

COLD AIR
WATER

The heat penetrates into deeper layers thanks to the transparency of the water. A part of the heat is lost in evaporation of the water.

2 **ON THE LAND**
During the evening, the land radiates away its heat more rapidly than the water. The difference in pressure generated replaces the cold air of the coast with warm air.

COLD AIR
LAND

When night falls, the land, which was hot, cools rapidly.

IN THE OCEAN
The loss of heat from the water is slower.

WARM AIR
WATER

When night falls, the water is lukewarm (barely a degree more than the land).

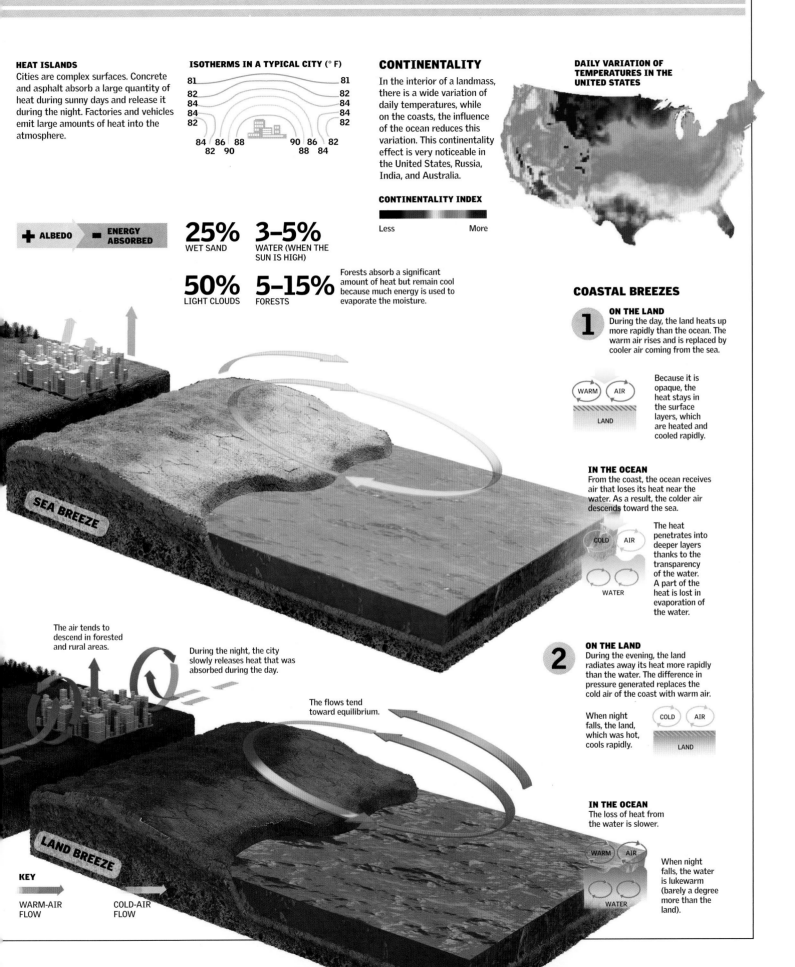

SEA BREEZE

The air tends to descend in forested and rural areas.

During the night, the city slowly releases heat that was absorbed during the day.

The flows tend toward equilibrium.

LAND BREEZE

KEY

→ WARM-AIR FLOW

→ COLD-AIR FLOW

The Rain Announces Its Coming

The air inside a cloud is in continuous motion. This process causes the drops of water or the crystals of ice that constitute the cloud to collide and join together. In the process, the drops or crystals become too big to be supported by air currents and they fall to the ground as different kinds of precipitation. A drop of rain may have a diameter 100 times greater than a water droplet in a cloud. The type of precipitation depends on whether the cloud contains drops of water, ice crystals, or both. Depending on the type of cloud and the temperature, the precipitation can be liquid water (rain) or solid (snow or hail).

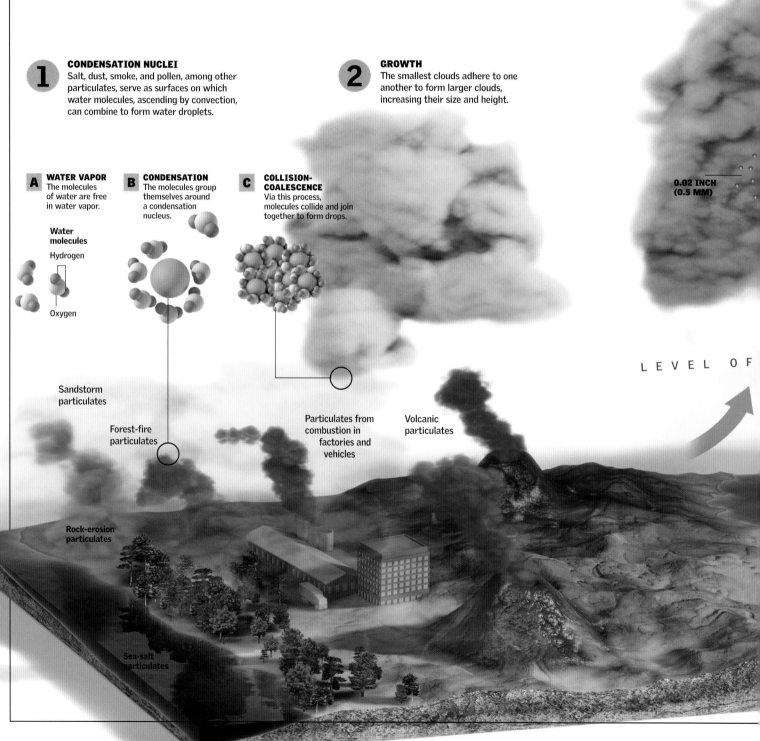

1 **CONDENSATION NUCLEI**
Salt, dust, smoke, and pollen, among other particulates, serve as surfaces on which water molecules, ascending by convection, can combine to form water droplets.

2 **GROWTH**
The smallest clouds adhere to one another to form larger clouds, increasing their size and height.

A **WATER VAPOR**
The molecules of water are free in water vapor.

B **CONDENSATION**
The molecules group themselves around a condensation nucleus.

C **COLLISION-COALESCENCE**
Via this process, molecules collide and join together to form drops.

0.02 INCH
(0.5 MM)

Water molecules

Hydrogen

Oxygen

LEVEL OF

Sandstorm particulates

Forest-fire particulates

Particulates from combustion in factories and vehicles

Volcanic particulates

Rock-erosion particulates

Sea-salt particulates

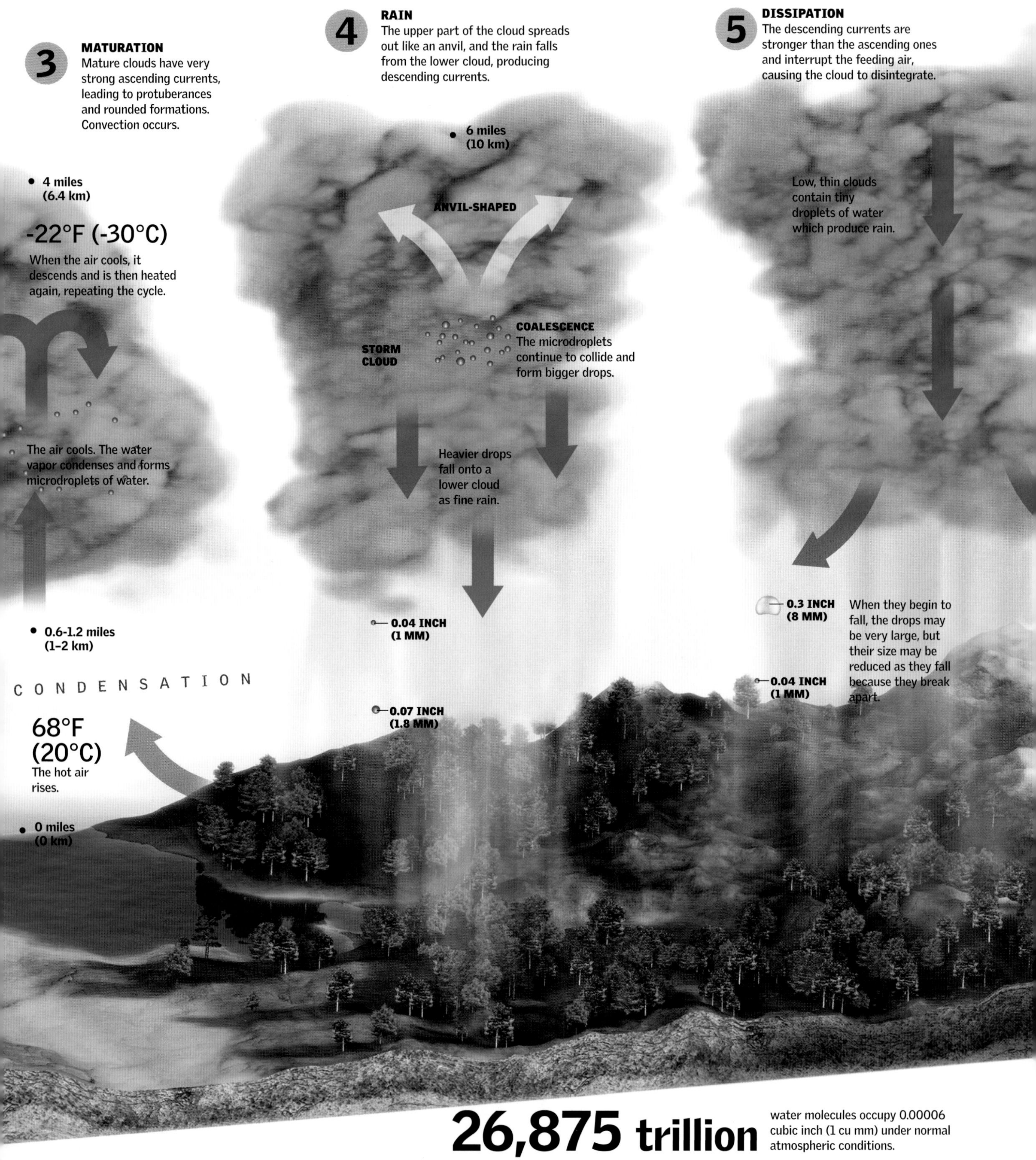

3 **MATURATION**
Mature clouds have very strong ascending currents, leading to protuberances and rounded formations. Convection occurs.

• 4 miles
(6.4 km)

-22°F (-30°C)
When the air cools, it descends and is then heated again, repeating the cycle.

The air cools. The water vapor condenses and forms microdroplets of water.

• 0.6-1.2 miles
(1-2 km)

C O N D E N S A T I O N

**68°F
(20°C)**
The hot air rises.

• 0 miles
(0 km)

4 **RAIN**
The upper part of the cloud spreads out like an anvil, and the rain falls from the lower cloud, producing descending currents.

• 6 miles
(10 km)

ANVIL-SHAPED

**STORM
CLOUD**

COALESCENCE
The microdroplets continue to collide and form bigger drops.

Heavier drops fall onto a lower cloud as fine rain.

◦— **0.04 INCH
(1 MM)**

◦— **0.07 INCH
(1.8 MM)**

5 **DISSIPATION**
The descending currents are stronger than the ascending ones and interrupt the feeding air, causing the cloud to disintegrate.

Low, thin clouds contain tiny droplets of water which produce rain.

◦— **0.3 INCH
(8 MM)**

When they begin to fall, the drops may be very large, but their size may be reduced as they fall because they break apart.

◦— **0.04 INCH
(1 MM)**

26,875 trillion water molecules occupy 0.00006 cubic inch (1 cu mm) under normal atmospheric conditions.

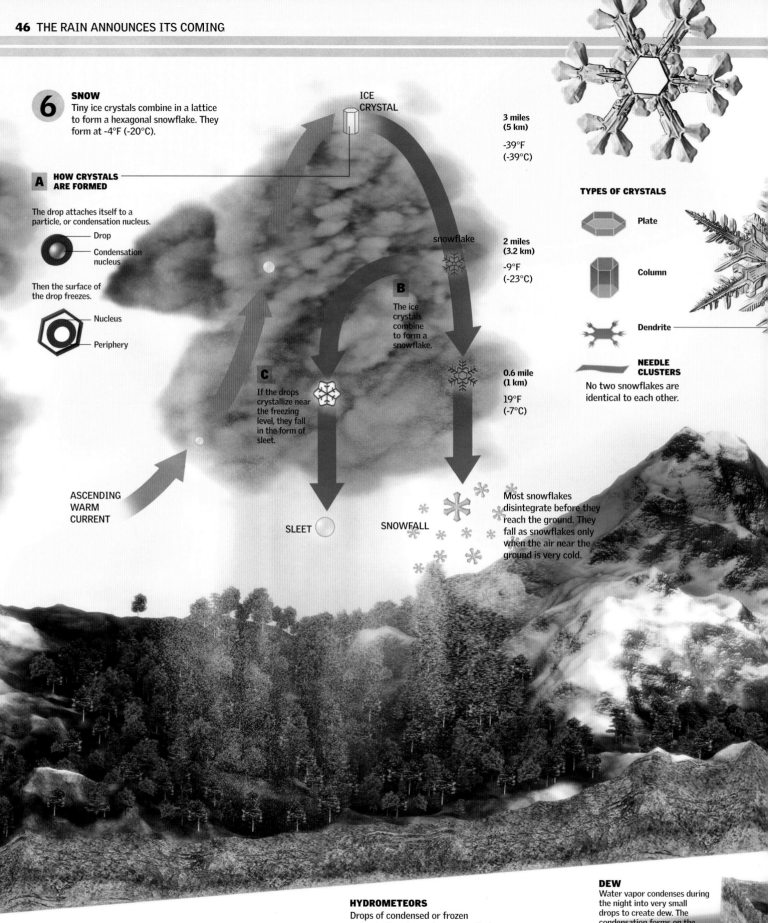

6 **SNOW**
Tiny ice crystals combine in a lattice to form a hexagonal snowflake. They form at -4°F (-20°C).

A **HOW CRYSTALS ARE FORMED**

The drop attaches itself to a particle, or condensation nucleus.

Drop
Condensation nucleus

Then the surface of the drop freezes.

Nucleus
Periphery

ICE CRYSTAL

snowflake

B
The ice crystals combine to form a snowflake.

C
If the drops crystallize near the freezing level, they fall in the form of sleet.

ASCENDING WARM CURRENT

SLEET

SNOWFALL

3 miles (5 km)
-39°F (-39°C)

2 miles (3.2 km)
-9°F (-23°C)

0.6 mile (1 km)
19°F (-7°C)

TYPES OF CRYSTALS

Plate

Column

Dendrite

NEEDLE CLUSTERS
No two snowflakes are identical to each other.

Most snowflakes disintegrate before they reach the ground. They fall as snowflakes only when the air near the ground is very cold.

HYDROMETEORS
Drops of condensed or frozen water in the atmosphere are called "hydrometeors." These include rain, fog, hail, mist, snow, and frost.

DEW
Water vapor condenses during the night into very small drops to create dew. The condensation forms on the ground and other surfaces that radiate heat at night, such as plants, animals, and buildings.

VARIED FORMS

Snow crystals have an infinite variety of shapes; most of them have six points, although some have twelve, and they have hexagonal symmetry in a plane. They can also be cubic crystals, but these form under conditions of extremely low temperature in the highest regions of the troposphere.

Snowflakes have six points.

The flakes measure between 0.04 and 0.8 inch (1 and 20 mm).

WARM ASCENDING CURRENT

A
Vertical air currents cause the microdroplets to ascend and descend within the cloud.

A cloud with a greenish tinge or rain with a whitish color can portend a hailstorm.

B
The droplets freeze, and each time they are carried upward in the cloud, they acquire a new layer of ice. This process, called "accretion," increases the size of the hailstone.

Soft hail, formed when droplets freeze on a falling snowflake, is also called snow pellets.

C
When the hailstones are too heavy to be supported by the ascending air currents, they fall to the ground.

7 HAIL
Precipitation in the form of solid lumps of ice. Hail is produced inside storm clouds in which frozen droplets grow in size as they rise and fall within the cloud.

CROSS SECTION OF A HAILSTONE

Layers of ice

0.2 TO 2 INCHES (5 TO 50 MM)
The typical range of hailstone sizes

2 pounds (1 kg) THE HEAVIEST HAILSTONES
THAT FELL ON APRIL 14, 1986, IN GOPALGANJ, BANGLADESH.

27°F (-3°C)
TEMPERATURE OF THE AIR

32°F (0°C)
DEW POINT

41°F (5°C)
TEMPERATURE OF THE GROUND

FROST
Frost forms when the dew point of the air is less than 32°F (0°C), and the water vapor transforms directly into ice when it is deposited on surfaces.

HOAR FROST
Similar to frost but thicker. It usually forms when there is fog.

DISCOVERY FACT™
The record for the highest annual snowfall on Mount Rainier, Washington State, is 93.5 ft (28.5 m), between July 1, 1971, and June 30, 1972.

Brief Flash

Electrical storms are produced in large cumulonimbus-type clouds, which typically bring heavy rains in addition to lightning and thunder. The storms form in areas of low pressure, where the air is warm and less dense than the surrounding atmosphere. Inside the cloud, an enormous electrical charge accumulates, which is then discharged with a zigzag flash between the cloud and the ground, between the cloud and the air, or between one cloud and another. This is how the flash of lightning is unleashed. At the same time, the heat that is released during the discharge generates an expansion and contraction of the air, which we hear as "thunder."

THUNDER
This is the sound produced by the air when it expands very rapidly, generating shock waves as it is heated.

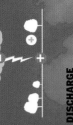

Cold air   Very hot air   Very hot air   Cold air

Cold air

Warm air

1 ORIGIN
Lightning originates within large cumulonimbus storm clouds. Lightning bolts can have negative or positive electrical charges.

TYPES OF LIGHTNING
Lightning can be distinguished primarily by the path taken by the electrical charges that cause them.

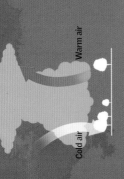

CLOUD-TO-AIR
The electricity moves from the cloud toward an air mass of opposite charge.

CLOUD-TO-CLOUD
A lightning flash can occur within a cloud or between two oppositely charged areas.

CLOUD-TO-GROUND
Negative charges of the cloud are attracted by the positive charges of the ground.

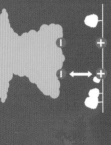

2 INSIDE THE CLOUD
Electrical charges are produced from the collisions between ice or hail crystals. Warm air currents rise, causing the charges in the cloud to shift.

SEPARATION
The charges become separated, with the positive charges accumulating at the top of the cloud and the negative charges at the base.

3 ELECTRICAL CHARGES
The cloud's negative charges are attracted to the positive charges of the ground. The difference in electrical potential between the two regions produces the discharge.

INDUCED CHARGE
The negative charge of the base of the cloud induces a positive charge in the ground below it.

4 DISCHARGE
The discharge takes place from the cloud toward the ground when a channel of ionized air, called a "leader," extends down to the ground. This characteristically splits and branches as it travels, when it is known as a "stepped leader."

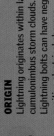

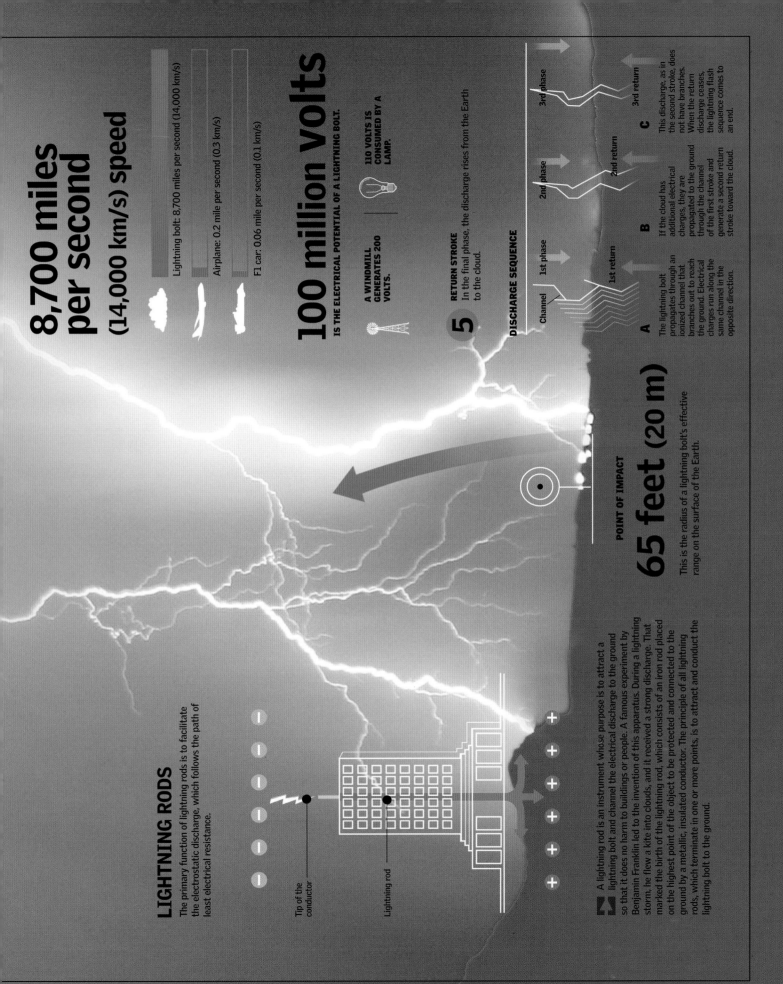

8,700 miles per second (14,000 km/s) speed

- Lightning bolt: 8,700 miles per second (14,000 km/s)
- Airplane: 0.2 mile per second (0.3 km/s)
- F1 car: 0.06 mile per second (0.1 km/s)

100 million volts

IS THE ELECTRICAL POTENTIAL OF A LIGHTNING BOLT.

110 VOLTS IS CONSUMED BY A LAMP.

A WINDMILL GENERATES 200 VOLTS.

5 RETURN STROKE
In the final phase, the discharge rises from the Earth to the cloud.

DISCHARGE SEQUENCE

Channel · 1st phase · 2nd phase · 3rd phase

1st return · 2nd return · 3rd return

A The lightning bolt propagates through an ionized channel that branches out to reach the ground. Electrical charges run along the same channel in the opposite direction.

B If the cloud has additional electrical charges, they are propagated to the ground through the channel of the first stroke and generate a second return stroke toward the cloud.

C This discharge, as in the second stroke, does not have branches. When the return discharge ceases, the lightning flash sequence comes to an end.

POINT OF IMPACT

65 feet (20 m)

This is the radius of a lightning bolt's effective range on the surface of the Earth.

LIGHTNING RODS

The primary function of lightning rods is to facilitate the electrostatic discharge, which follows the path of least electrical resistance.

Tip of the conductor

Lightning rod

A lightning rod is an instrument whose purpose is to attract a lightning bolt and channel the electrical discharge to the ground so that it does no harm to buildings or people. A famous experiment by Benjamin Franklin led to the invention of this apparatus. During a lightning storm, he flew a kite into clouds, and it received a strong discharge. That marked the birth of the lightning rod, which consists of an iron rod placed on the highest point of the object to be protected and connected to the ground by a metallic, insulated conductor. The principle of all lightning rods, which terminate in one or more points, is to attract and conduct the lightning bolt to the ground.

Anatomy of a Hurricane

A hurricane, with its ferocious winds, banks of clouds, and torrential rains, is the Earth's most spectacular meteorological phenomenon. It is characterized by an intense low-pressure center surrounded by cloud bands arranged in spiral form; these rotate around the eye of the hurricane in a clockwise direction in the Southern Hemisphere and in the opposite direction in the Northern Hemisphere. While tornadoes are brief and relatively limited, hurricanes are enormous and slow-moving, and their passage usually takes many lives.

DAY 1
A jumble of clouds is formed.

1

BIRTH
The hurricane forms over warm seas, aided by winds in opposing directions, high temperatures, humidity, and the rotation of the Earth.

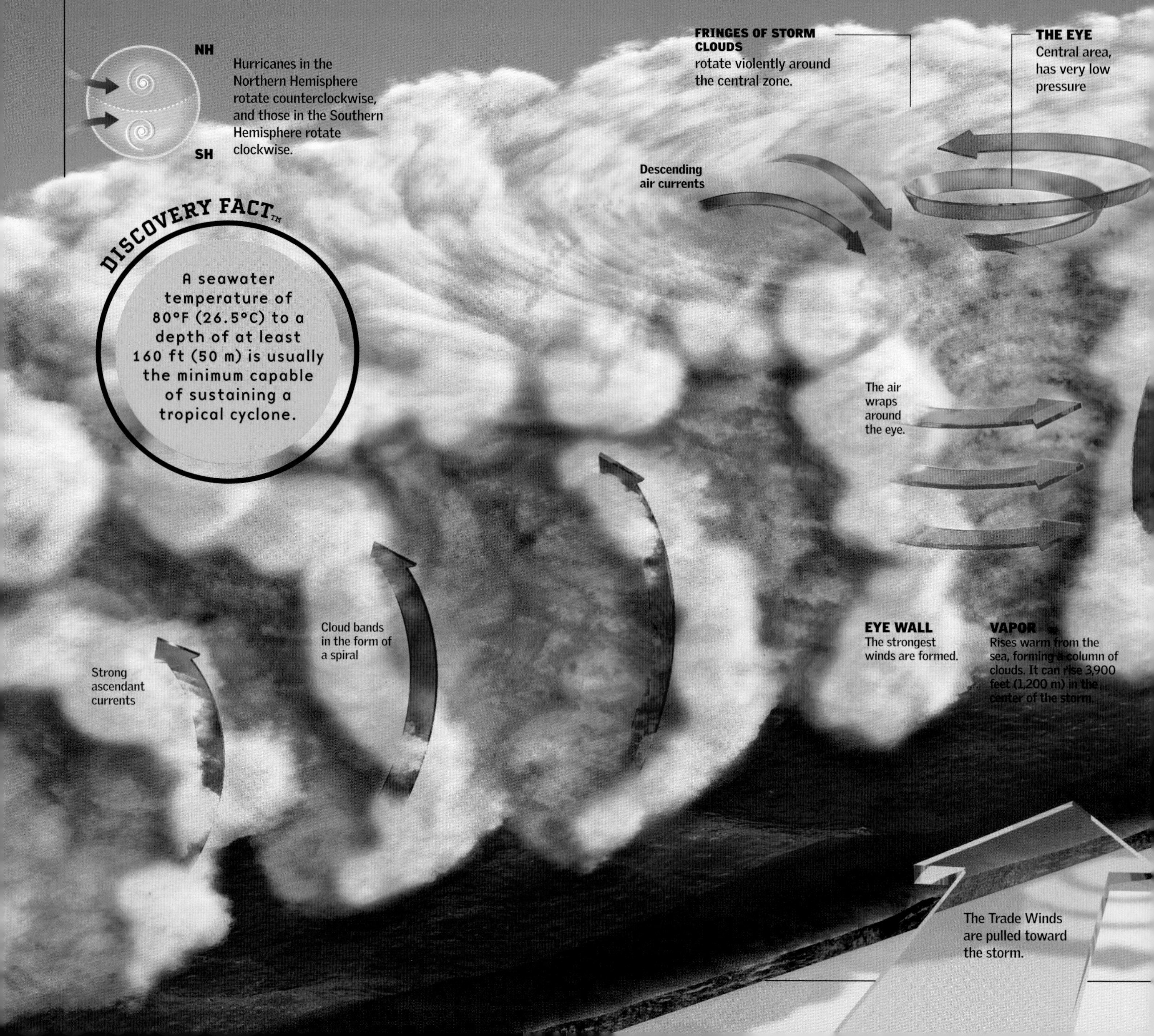

NH

SH

Hurricanes in the Northern Hemisphere rotate counterclockwise, and those in the Southern Hemisphere rotate clockwise.

FRINGES OF STORM CLOUDS
rotate violently around the central zone.

THE EYE
Central area, has very low pressure

Descending air currents

DISCOVERY FACT™

A seawater temperature of 80°F (26.5°C) to a depth of at least 160 ft (50 m) is usually the minimum capable of sustaining a tropical cyclone.

The air wraps around the eye.

Strong ascendant currents

Cloud bands in the form of a spiral

EYE WALL
The strongest winds are formed.

VAPOR
Rises warm from the sea, forming a column of clouds. It can rise 3,900 feet (1,200 m) in the center of the storm.

The Trade Winds are pulled toward the storm.

DAY 2
The clouds begin to rotate.

DAY 3
The spiral form becomes more defined.

HURRICANE
TYPHOON
Equator
CYCLONE

DANGER ZONE
The areas that are vulnerable to hurricanes in the United States include the Atlantic coast and the coast along the Gulf of Mexico, from Texas to Maine. The Caribbean and the tropical areas of the western Pacific, including Hawaii, Guam, American Samoa, and Saipan, are also zones frequented by hurricanes.

DAY 6
Now mature, it displays a visible eye.

DAY 12
The hurricane begins to break apart when it makes landfall.

2 DEVELOPMENT
It begins to ascend, twisting in a spiral around a low-pressure zone.

19 miles per hour (30 km/h)
VELOCITY AT WHICH IT APPROACHES THE COAST

FRICTION
When the hurricane reaches the mainland, it moves more slowly; it is very destructive in this stage, since it is here that populated cities are located.

3 DEATH
As it passes from the sea to the land, it causes enormous damage. Hurricanes gradually dissipate over land from a lack of water vapor.

The high-altitude winds blow from outside the storm.

PATH OF THE HURRICANE

100 feet (30 m)
MAXIMUM HEIGHT REACHED BY THE WAVES

1
2
3
4
5

CLASSIFICATION OF HURRICANES SCALE
Saffir-Simpson categories

	DAMAGE	SPEED miles per hour (km/h)	HIGH TIDE feet (m)
CLASS 1	**MINIMUM**	74–95 (119–153)	4–5 (1.2–1.5)
CLASS 2	**MODERATE**	96–110 (154–177)	6–8 (1.8–2.4)
CLASS 3	**EXTENSIVE**	111–130 (179–209)	9–12 (2.7–3.6)
CLASS 4	**EXTREME**	131–155 (211–250)	13–18 (4.0–5.5)
CLASS 5	**CATASTROPHIC**	More than 155 (250)	More than 18 (5.5)

WIND ACTIVITY

Light winds give it direction and permit it to grow.

The winds flow outward.

Everything Changes

Wind, ice, and water—these natural elements cause great changes in the Earth's landscape. Erosion and transportation are processes that produce and spread rock materials. Then, when these materials settle and become compacted, new rocks are created, which in turn will revert to sediment. These are sedimentary rocks: the most widely known rocks, they cover 70 percent of the Earth's surface. By observing sedimentary rocks of different ages, scientists can estimate how the climate and the environment have changed.

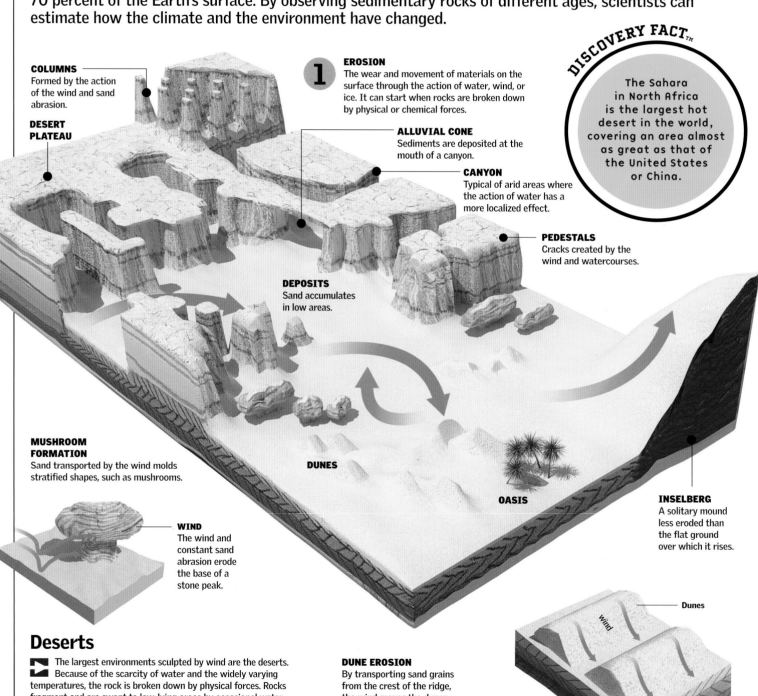

COLUMNS
Formed by the action of the wind and sand abrasion.

DESERT PLATEAU

1 EROSION
The wear and movement of materials on the surface through the action of water, wind, or ice. It can start when rocks are broken down by physical or chemical forces.

ALLUVIAL CONE
Sediments are deposited at the mouth of a canyon.

CANYON
Typical of arid areas where the action of water has a more localized effect.

PEDESTALS
Cracks created by the wind and watercourses.

DEPOSITS
Sand accumulates in low areas.

DISCOVERY FACT™

The Sahara in North Africa is the largest hot desert in the world, covering an area almost as great as that of the United States or China.

MUSHROOM FORMATION
Sand transported by the wind molds stratified shapes, such as mushrooms.

DUNES

OASIS

INSELBERG
A solitary mound less eroded than the flat ground over which it rises.

WIND
The wind and constant sand abrasion erode the base of a stone peak.

Deserts

The largest environments sculpted by wind are the deserts. Because of the scarcity of water and the widely varying temperatures, the rock is broken down by physical forces. Rocks fragment and are swept to low-lying areas by occasional water currents. Then sand and mud will be swept away by the wind in a process called "deflation." Through this process particles can be transported into semiarid regions.

DUNE EROSION
By transporting sand grains from the crest of the ridge, the wind moves the dunes. The grains can be transported up to 100 feet (30 m) per year.

Dunes

wind

ACCUMULATED SEDIMENTS

TRANSPORTATION OF SEDIMENTS

DESERT
TINY GRAINS
In the desert, the wind moves particles in three ways: suspension (very fine grains and dust), transportation (the most basic way), and sliding along the surface.

SAND

WIND

3 INCHES
(7.5 CM)

GLACIER
FINE AND HETEROGENEOUS
Glaciers transport rock fragments, which accumulate in moraines. They are made up of a heterogeneous material called "till," which, together with rocks, is carried along by the glacier.

ICE

TILL

160 FEET
(50 M)

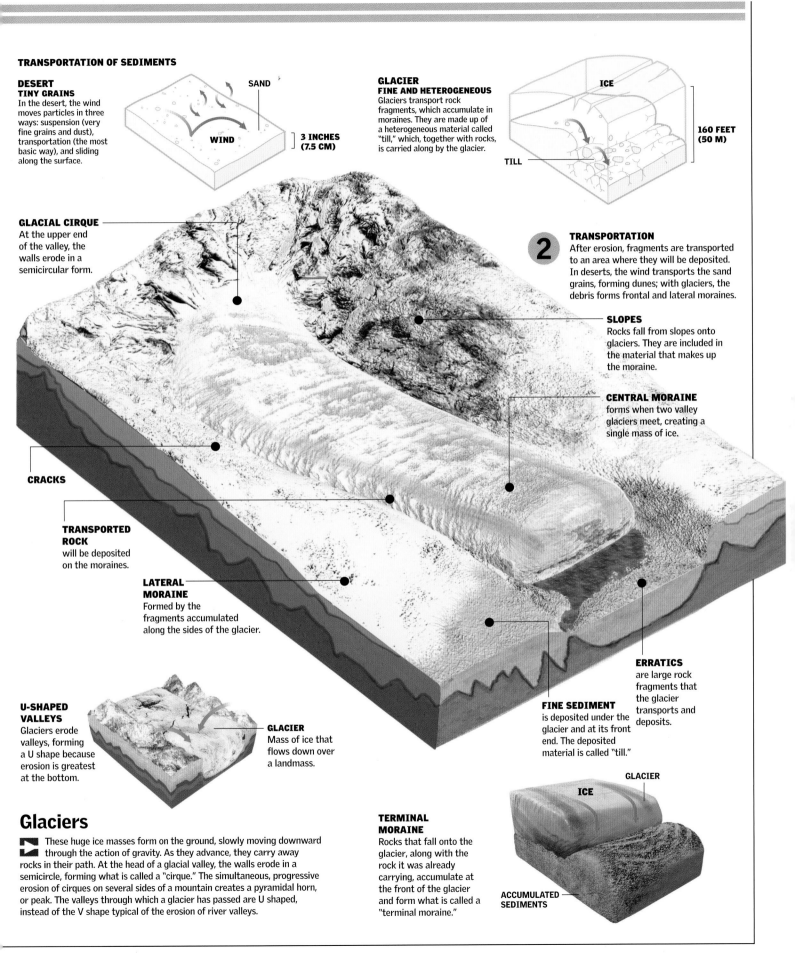

GLACIAL CIRQUE
At the upper end of the valley, the walls erode in a semicircular form.

2 TRANSPORTATION
After erosion, fragments are transported to an area where they will be deposited. In deserts, the wind transports the sand grains, forming dunes; with glaciers, the debris forms frontal and lateral moraines.

SLOPES
Rocks fall from slopes onto glaciers. They are included in the material that makes up the moraine.

CENTRAL MORAINE
forms when two valley glaciers meet, creating a single mass of ice.

CRACKS

TRANSPORTED ROCK
will be deposited on the moraines.

LATERAL MORAINE
Formed by the fragments accumulated along the sides of the glacier.

ERRATICS
are large rock fragments that the glacier transports and deposits.

U-SHAPED VALLEYS
Glaciers erode valleys, forming a U shape because erosion is greatest at the bottom.

GLACIER
Mass of ice that flows down over a landmass.

FINE SEDIMENT
is deposited under the glacier and at its front end. The deposited material is called "till."

Glaciers

These huge ice masses form on the ground, slowly moving downward through the action of gravity. As they advance, they carry away rocks in their path. At the head of a glacial valley, the walls erode in a semicircle, forming what is called a "cirque." The simultaneous, progressive erosion of cirques on several sides of a mountain creates a pyramidal horn, or peak. The valleys through which a glacier has passed are U shaped, instead of the V shape typical of the erosion of river valleys.

TERMINAL MORAINE
Rocks that fall onto the glacier, along with the rock it was already carrying, accumulate at the front of the glacier and form what is called a "terminal moraine."

GLACIER
ICE

ACCUMULATED SEDIMENTS

TRANSPORTATION OF SEDIMENTS

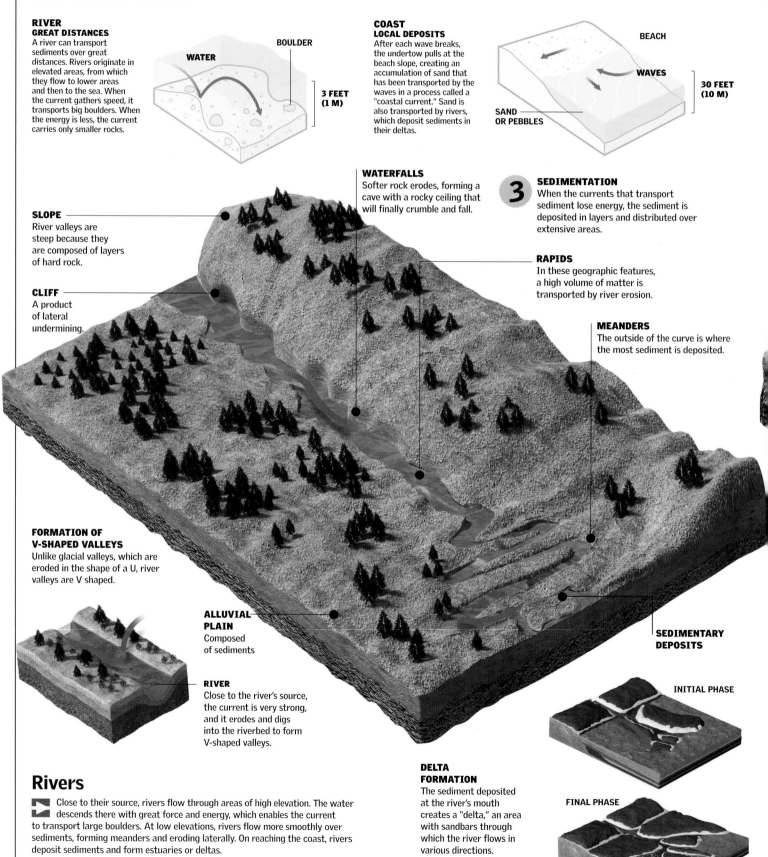

**RIVER
GREAT DISTANCES**
A river can transport sediments over great distances. Rivers originate in elevated areas, from which they flow to lower areas and then to the sea. When the current gathers speed, it transports big boulders. When the energy is less, the current carries only smaller rocks.

WATER

BOULDER

**3 FEET
(1 M)**

**COAST
LOCAL DEPOSITS**
After each wave breaks, the undertow pulls at the beach slope, creating an accumulation of sand that has been transported by the waves in a process called a "coastal current." Sand is also transported by rivers, which deposit sediments in their deltas.

BEACH

WAVES

**30 FEET
(10 M)**

**SAND
OR PEBBLES**

SLOPE
River valleys are steep because they are composed of layers of hard rock.

CLIFF
A product of lateral undermining.

WATERFALLS
Softer rock erodes, forming a cave with a rocky ceiling that will finally crumble and fall.

3 **SEDIMENTATION**
When the currents that transport sediment lose energy, the sediment is deposited in layers and distributed over extensive areas.

RAPIDS
In these geographic features, a high volume of matter is transported by river erosion.

MEANDERS
The outside of the curve is where the most sediment is deposited.

**FORMATION OF
V-SHAPED VALLEYS**
Unlike glacial valleys, which are eroded in the shape of a U, river valleys are V shaped.

**ALLUVIAL
PLAIN**
Composed of sediments

RIVER
Close to the river's source, the current is very strong, and it erodes and digs into the riverbed to form V-shaped valleys.

**SEDIMENTARY
DEPOSITS**

INITIAL PHASE

FINAL PHASE

Rivers

Close to their source, rivers flow through areas of high elevation. The water descends there with great force and energy, which enables the current to transport large boulders. At low elevations, rivers flow more smoothly over sediments, forming meanders and eroding laterally. On reaching the coast, rivers deposit sediments and form estuaries or deltas.

**DELTA
FORMATION**
The sediment deposited at the river's mouth creates a "delta," an area with sandbars through which the river flows in various directions.

CEMENTATION PROCESS

This is the most important process that transforms sediment into rock. Cementation occurs when particles join with the materials precipitated from the water currents. Sedimentary rocks are formed through the union of different minerals that have been dissolved in water. When the water evaporates or cools, the dissolved minerals precipitate and form deposits that accumulate with other sediments, or they can form rocks on their own. Salts and sandstone are common examples of cemented rocks.

SEPARATION
BY WEIGHT

MINERAL
DEPOSITS

COASTAL PLAIN

An area of low-lying land that usually lies inland from a beach and may once have been under the sea as part of the continental shelf.

4 COMPACTION

The successive layers of sedimentary deposits compact the lower ones by exerting pressure on them, in a process known as "lithification," which forms new rock.

MARINE ABRASION PLATFORM

Shelved area created by tidal action indicating a previous, higher shoreline.

CAVE

Caves are cut into the rock through abrasion.

SOLID
ROCK

CLIFFS

originate through the erosive action of the waves against the base of coastal terrain.

ESTUARY

Former river valley that is now flooded. It offers the necessary conditions for depositing large amounts of sediment.

SEDIMENTARY DEPOSIT

An accumulation of sediments transported by longshore (coastal) drift.

CONTINENTAL SHELF

Sedimentary deposits may contribute to the underwater landmass that results in a shallow area known as a "shelf sea."

RECEDING COASTLINE

Along the coast, the effects of erosion caused by waves are easy to spot. Cliffs are created through the erosive action of the waves against the base of coastal terrain. As the erosion progresses, the undermining of the cliff's base leaves higher rock layers jutting outward, which then collapse. The cliff recedes, and the debris may be carried away by the action of the sea.

Coasts

Ocean coasts are the most changing landscapes in the Earth's geography, thanks to a process called "coastal drift." The elements that build up the coastline—wind, rain, and waves—also erode and mold it. Thus, the waves that bring the sediments that form beaches and carry them away are the same waves that can create or knock down a cliff or cave. Its remnants will be the building material for another beach, along with the sediment that comes from rivers and their deltas.

BEACH FORMATION

Beaches are formed from the gradual deposits of waves in low-energy coastal zones. They can be made of fine sediment, such as sand, or larger materials, such as gravel or pebbles.

WAVES

ACCUMULATED
SEDIMENTS

Metamorphic Processes

When rocks are subjected to certain conditions (high pressure and temperature or exposure to fluids with dissolved chemicals), they can undergo remarkable changes in both their mineral composition and their structure. This very slow process, called "metamorphism," is a veritable transformation of the rock. The phenomenon originates inside the Earth's crust as well as on the surface. The type of metamorphism depends on the nature of the energy that triggers the change. This energy can be heat or pressure.

SCOTLAND,
UNITED KINGDOM
Latitude   57° N
Longitude   04° W

Scotland was raised in the Caledonian orogeny 400 million years ago. This pressure produced the gneiss shown in the photo.

DISCOVERY FACT™

Gneiss is often "foliated," or composed of layers of different minerals, which give it a striped appearance when it is broken and seen from the side.

Dynamic Metamorphism

The least common type of metamorphism, dynamic metamorphism happens when the large-scale movement of the crust along fault systems causes the rocks to be compressed. Great rock masses thrust over others. Where they come in contact, new metamorphic rocks, called "cataclasites" and "mylonites," are formed.

2

● Schist

SLATE
In environments with high temperature and pressure, slates will become "phyllites."

570°F
(300°C)
SLATE
Low-grade metamorphic rock formed from mudstone or shale in which the clay is transformed into mica minerals.

930°F
(500°C)
SCHIST
Very flaky rock produced by metamorphism at intermediate temperatures and depths greater than 6 miles (10 km). The minerals form into large crystals that give it luster.

1,200°F
(650°C)
GNEISS
Produced through highly metamorphic processes more than 12 miles (20 km) beneath the surface, it involves extremely powerful tectonic forces and temperatures near the melting point of rock.

1,470°F
(800°C)
FUSION
At this temperature, most rocks start to melt until they become liquid.

Regional Metamorphism
As mountains form, a large amount of rock is deformed and transformed. Rocks buried close to the surface descend to greater depths and are modified by higher temperatures and pressures. This metamorphism covers thousands of square miles and is classified according to the temperature and pressure reached. Slate is an example of rock affected by this type of process.

1

Intermediate Crust

Lower Crust

PRESSURE
As the pressure increases on the rocks, the mineralogical structure of rocks is reorganized, which reduces their size.

Contact Metamorphism
Magmatic rocks transmit heat, so a body of magma can heat rocks on contact. The affected area, located around an igneous intrusion or lava flow, is called an "aureole." Its size depends on the intrusion and on the magma's temperature. The minerals of the surrounding rock turn into other minerals, and the rock metamorphoses.

1

Sandstone

Schist

Limestone — Magma

2

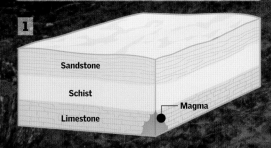

Quarzite

Hornfels — Magma

Marble

TEMPERATURE
The closer the rock is to the heat source and the greater the temperature, the higher is the degree of metamorphism that takes place.

The Basis of Life

Organisms are born, live, reproduce, and die on a natural layer of soil. From this layer, crops are harvested, livestock are raised, and construction materials are obtained. It establishes the link between life and the mineral part of the planet. Through the action of climate and biological agents, soil forms where rocks are broken down.

DISCOVERY FACT™

Depending on climate and rock type, between 200 and 1,000 years are needed for the natural formation of a 1-in (2.5-cm) layer of fertile soil.

Types of Soil

Soil consists of bedrock materials that have been greatly altered by air and water, together with living organisms and decomposed organic materials. The many physical and chemical transformations that the material undergoes produce different types of soil, some richer in humus, others with more clay, and so on. The soil's basic texture depends to a great extent on the type of bedrock from which it is formed.

RANKERS
These soils develop on top of slightly altered bedrock. They are typical in high mountains, especially if they form on granite or other acidic rocks.

0.2%
of the world's land surface

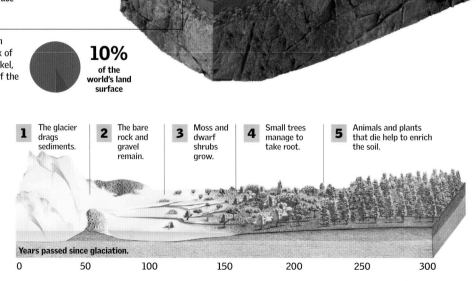

PERMAFROST
Areas near the poles. The soil is saturated with frozen water. In the parts that thaw, big puddles are formed. Because of its characteristics, many animals cannot live there.

20%
of the world's land surface

DESERTIC
Arid soil. Containing very little humus, it rests directly on mineral deposits and rock fragments.

14%
of the world's land surface

LATERITE
Typical tropical soil. With abundant rains and humidity in these zones, the soil is well drained. The rain leaves a mix of oxides and hydroxides of aluminum, iron, manganese, nickel, and other minerals in the soil. It represents 70 percent of the world's iron reserves.

10%
of the world's land surface

HOW IT FORMS
Much of the Earth's crust is covered with a layer of sediment and decomposing organic matter. This layer, called "soil," covers everything except very steep slopes. Although it is created from decomposing plant and animal remains, the soil is a living and changing system. Its tiniest cavities, home to thousands of bacteria, algae, and fungi, are filled with water or air. These microorganisms speed up the decomposition process, turning the soil into a habitat favorable to plant roots as well as small animals and insects.

1 The glacier drags sediments.

2 The bare rock and gravel remain.

3 Moss and dwarf shrubs grow.

4 Small trees manage to take root.

5 Animals and plants that die help to enrich the soil.

Years passed since glaciation.

0   50   100   150   200   250   300

Different Characteristics

Observing the soil profile makes it possible to distinguish layers called "horizons." Each layer has different characteristics and properties, hence the importance of identifying the layers to study and describe them. The surface layer is rich in organic matter. Beneath is the subsoil, where nutrients accumulate and some roots penetrate. Deeper down is a layer of rocks and pebbles.

UPPER LAYER
This layer is dark and rich in nutrients. It contains a network of plant roots along with humus, which is formed from plant and animal residues.

SUBSOIL
contains many mineral particles from the bedrock. It is formed by complex humus.

BEDROCK
The continuous breakdown and erosion of the bedrock helps increase the thickness of the soil. Soil texture also depends to a great extent on the type of bedrock on which it forms.

- 0
- 3 ft (1 m)
- 7 ft (2 m)
- 10 ft (3 m)

Living Organisms in the Soil

Many bacteria and fungi live in the soil; their biomass usually surpasses that of all animals living on the surface. Algae (mainly diatoms) also live closest to the surface, where there is most light. Mites, springtails, insect larvae, earthworms, and others are also found there. Earthworms build tunnels that aerate the soil and make the growth of roots easier. Their droppings retain water and contain important nutrients.

EARTHWORMS
It takes approximately 6,000 earthworms to produce 3,000 pounds (1,360 kg) of humus.

HUMUS
is the substance composed of organic materials, usually found in the upper layers of soil. It is produced by microorganisms, mainly acting on fallen vegetation and animal droppings. The dark color of this highly fertile layer comes from its high carbon content.

Rock Cycle

Some rocks go through the rock cycle to form soil. Under the action of erosive agents, rocks from the Earth's crust take on characteristic shapes. These shapes are a consequence partly of the rock's own composition and partly of several effects caused by erosive agents (meteorological and biological) responsible for breaking down rocky material.

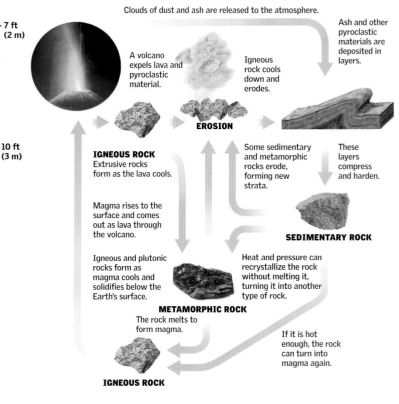

Clouds of dust and ash are released to the atmosphere.

A volcano expels lava and pyroclastic material.

Igneous rock cools down and erodes.

Ash and other pyroclastic materials are deposited in layers.

EROSION

IGNEOUS ROCK
Extrusive rocks form as the lava cools.

Some sedimentary and metamorphic rocks erode, forming new strata.

These layers compress and harden.

Magma rises to the surface and comes out as lava through the volcano.

SEDIMENTARY ROCK

Igneous and plutonic rocks form as magma cools and solidifies below the Earth's surface.

Heat and pressure can recrystallize the rock without melting it, turning it into another type of rock.

METAMORPHIC ROCK
The rock melts to form magma.

If it is hot enough, the rock can turn into magma again.

IGNEOUS ROCK

Kingdoms of Quiet Life

Representing a vast array of life-forms, the plant kingdom includes approximately 300,000 species. Their outstanding feature is the presence of chloroplasts with chlorophyll, a pigment that enables them to transform solar energy into chemical energy, which they use to produce their food. Plants need to attach themselves to a substrate (usually soil), from which they can extract water and nutrients. Thus immobilized, they need to adapt to survive different conditions in their environment. Algae and fungi were once included in the plant kingdom, but are now considered to be separate from plants: they belong to the kingdoms Protista and Fungi, respectively.

MOSS
Sphagnum sp.

RED MARINE ALGA
Rhodomela sp.

Algae

Living in water (freshwater or saltwater), algae need no substrate, and lack the structures typical of plants, such as roots and leaves. Algae are a very large and diverse group, ranging from large seaweeds to unicellular species, some of which may multiply rapidly into very large formations, or "blooms." Green algae are characterized by having chloroplasts, which photosynthesize chlorophyll, and by storing energy in the form of starch, like plants.

Bryophytes

These include mosses, hornworts, and liverworts. They can also absorb water through their entire body surface, but have no system of veins for transporting nutrients, so can barely grow beyond 0.4 inch (1 cm) long. Bryophytes lack a means of functioning during drought, so when dry periods come, they enter a latent state. They produce neither seeds nor flowers, reproducing via spores.

Plants

The plant kingdom (Plantae) includes organisms whose characteristics include the presence of the pigment chlorophyll to convert solar energy into chemical energy for producing food from water and carbon dioxide. This ability is called "autotrophy." All plants, whether large or small, play an extremely important role in providing food for all other living beings. Plants cannot move from place to place, but their gametes, spores (cells that separate from a plant and can germinate), and seeds can move about, usually with the help of water and wind.

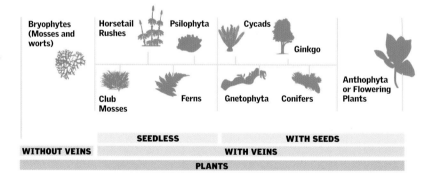

		SEEDLESS			WITH SEEDS	
Bryophytes (Mosses and worts)	Horsetail Rushes / Psilophyta	Cycads / Ginkgo	Anthophyta or Flowering Plants
Green Algae	Club Mosses / Ferns	Gnetophyta / Conifers	
WITHOUT VEINS	**WITH VEINS**		
	PLANTS		

FERN
Osmunda sp.

Seedless

Ferns are the most common seedless plants today. Many are thought to have originated during the Devonian Period and reached their greatest splendor in the Carboniferous Period. Their tissues are simpler than those of plants with seeds, and their green stems have a large surface area, giving them a great capacity for photosynthesis. Ferns need water so that they can reproduce by means of spores. The spores are produced in spore cases, called "sporangia," which grow on leaves called "sporophylls."

FERNS
are the most diverse group of seedless plants, with about 12,000 species.

SPIKE MOSS
has scalelike leaves, some of which are clustered in the form of a spike.

PSILOPHYTA
are extremely simple plants; they lack roots and true leaves, but they have stems with veins.

HORSETAIL RUSHES
have roots, stems, and true leaves. The leaves are small and encircle the stems.

CONIFERS

are the most abundant plants with seeds today. Their reproductive structures are called "cones." Most conifers are evergreens.

CYCADS

are tropical plants that look like palm trees. Their reproduction is similar to that of pines, but they are dioecious (each plant having flowers of only one sex).

GINKGOS

Only one species is left in this group, the oldest genus of living trees.

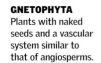

GNETOPHYTA

Plants with naked seeds and a vascular system similar to that of angiosperms.

Gymnosperma

The Greek word means "naked seed." Gymnosperms are vascular plants with exposed seeds and no flowers. Ginkgos (Ginkgophyta) and cycads (Cycadophyta) were the most common plant groups in ancient times. Today, conifers (such as pines, larches, cypresses, and firs) are the most common type. Conifers are "monoecious"—that is, the same plant carries both male and female sexual organs—and their seeds are held between the scales of a structure called a "cone."

SITKA SPRUCE
Picea sitchensis

Fungi

Unlike plants, fungi do not carry out photosynthesis, and they store energy in the form of glycogen rather than starch. Fungi are "heterotrophic" (they get their food from other organisms), and they take in food by absorption. Fungi can be either parasitic or feed on dead organic material. Some fungi are microscopic; others are large and conspicuous. Their bodies are composed of mycelium, a mass of filaments called "hyphae," and some fungi also have a fruit-bearing structure.

WHITE MUSHROOM
Agaricus bisporus

WHEAT
Triticum sp.

CHRISTMAS ORCHID
Cattleya trianae

ORCHIDS

Their number of petals is always a multiple of three. There are over 20,000 species making them the largest group of monocotyledons.

Angiosperms

These plants have seeds, flowers, and fruit. They include more than 250,000 species and are adapted to nearly all environments except for Antarctica. They reproduce sexually by producing flowers that later form fruits with seeds. Angiosperms have an efficient vascular system for transporting water (through the xylem) and food (through the phloem). They make up a division of the plant kingdom that includes plants with bright flowers; grains, such as rice and wheat; other crops, such as cotton, tobacco, and coffee; and trees, such as oak, cherry, and chestnut.

CEREALS

are monocotyledons. Their seeds have only one cotyledon (embryonic leaf), and their mature leaves have parallel veins.

Aquatic Plants

These plants are specially adapted to live in ponds, lakes, and rivers—where other plants cannot grow. Although they belong to many different families, they have similar adaptations and are therefore examples of "adaptive convergence." They include submerged and floating plants; amphibious plants, which have leaves both above and below the surface; and heliophilic plants, which have only their roots underwater.

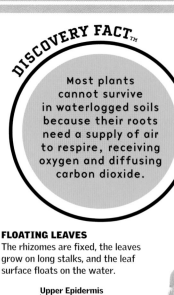

DISCOVERY FACT™

Most plants cannot survive in waterlogged soils because their roots need a supply of air to respire, receiving oxygen and diffusing carbon dioxide.

A Vital Role

Aquatic plants play an important role in the ecosystem. They are a source of food and shelter not only for crustaceans, insects, and worms but also for fish, birds, and mammals, converting solar energy into the organic materials upon which many living things depend.

PARROTFEATHER
Myriophyllum aquaticum
Native to temperate, subtropical, and tropical regions, it is highly effective at oxygenating water.

Rooted Plants with Floating Leaves

Such plants are often found in standing or slow-moving water. They have fixed rhizomes and petiolate leaves (leaves with a stalk that connects to a stem) which float on the surface of the water. Some species have submerged leaves, some have floating leaves, and some have leaves outside the water, with each type having a different shape. In the case of floating leaves, the properties of the upper surface are different from those of the lower surface, which is in contact with the water.

VICTORIA LILY
Victoria amazonica
It grows in shallow, calm waters of the Amazon basin. Its floating leaves measure up to 10 feet (3 m) across.

FLOATING LEAVES
The rhizomes are fixed, the leaves grow on long stalks, and the leaf surface floats on the water.

Upper Epidermis
Parenchyma
Aerenchyma
Lower Epidermis
Conduction Bundle
Air Chamber

YELLOW FLOATING HEART
Nymphoides peltata
It produces small creased yellow flowers all summer long.

Rooted Underwater Plants

The entire plant is submerged. The small root system serves only to anchor the plant, since the stem can directly absorb water, carbon dioxide, and minerals. These plants are often found in flowing water. The submerged stems have no system of support—the water holds the plant up.

HORNWORT
Ceratophyllum sp.
This plant has an abundance of fine leaves that form a conelike structure on each stem.

They produce and release oxygen as a result of photosynthesis.

SAGO PONDWEED
Potamogeton densus
This water plant can be found in shallow depressions of clear-flowing streams.

Aquatic but Modern

The evolutionary history of plants began in water environments. They later conquered land by means of structures such as roots. Modern aquatic plants are not a primitive group, however. On the contrary, they have returned to the water environment by acquiring highly specialized organs and tissues. For example, some tissues have air pockets that enable the plant to float.

Aerenchyma

is always found in floating organisms. This tissue has an extensive system of intercellular spaces through which gases are diffused.

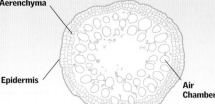

Aerenchyma
Epidermis
Air Chamber

Submerged stems have no support system because the water holds up the plant. Their limiting factor is oxygen availability, so the aerenchyma helps make this substance available to the plant.

Amphibious or Wetland Plants

These species live on the edges of ponds, rivers, and swamps. They are also found in salt marshes, which are periodically flooded by tides or river overflows. These plants are a transition between aquatic and land plants. Their limiting factor is the availability of oxygen, so they have well-developed aerenchyma.

300 THE NUMBER OF WELL-KNOWN SPECIES OF WATER PLANTS

CATTAILS
Typha sp.
grow in moist soil, around lake margins, and in marshes, in both temperate and tropical climates.

GREEN CAPE COWSLIP
Lachenalia viridiflora
This plant is attractive, with a large number of flowers.

Aquatic plant with especially beautiful flowers.

ARROWHEAD
Sagittaria sagittifolia
Its flowers, with three white petals and purple stamens, form during the summer.

The roots and rhizomes under the water are well developed.

KNOTWEED
Polygonum sp.
This aquatic plant grows in marshy vegetation.

Pneumatophores

are floating roots that are involved in air exchange. They take oxygen from the surface, and it circulates to the rest of the plant through its intracellular spaces. They probably also allow carbon dioxide to escape. Certain plants have a special adaptation that consists of air sacs that store oxygen for periods when the plant will be submerged or that speed up the plant's transpiration.

Submerged or Free

Some underwater plants are free, without roots, but with developed stalks and divided leaves. Other floating plants have a rosette shape and leaves modified for floating; they have well-developed roots with root caps but without absorbent hairs. The roots help the plant to stay balanced on top of the water.

BLADDERWORT
Utricularia vulgaris
These carnivorous plants complement their diet with small aquatic creatures.

The underwater parts do not have an impermeable outer layer, so they can absorb minerals and gases directly from the water.

EELGRASS
Vallisneria sp.
This oxygenating plant is often used in ponds and aquariums.

Conquest of Land

The movement of plants from shallow water onto land is associated with a series of evolutionary events. Certain changes in the genetic makeup of plants enabled them to face the new and extreme conditions found on the Earth's surface. Although land habitats offered plants direct exposure to sunlight, they also presented the problem of transpiration and the loss of water that it involves. This difficulty had to be overcome before plants could spread over land.

Vital Changes

Roots are among the most important adaptations for the success of plants in land habitats. Root systems anchor the plant in the substrate and serve as a pathway for water and mineral nutrients. As well as roots, the development of a cuticle (skin membrane) to cover the entire plant's surface was crucial. Cells in the epidermis produce this waterproof membrane, which helps the plant tolerate the heat generated by sunlight and the wear and loss of water caused by the wind. This protection is interrupted by pores, which allow for gas exchange.

Green Revolution

Leaves are the main organs for photosynthesis in land plants. After plants appeared on land more than 440 million years ago, the amount of photosynthesis taking place gradually increased. This increase is believed to be one of the reasons the concentration of carbon dioxide in the atmosphere decreased. As a result, the Earth's average temperature also fell.

MALE FERN
Dryopteris filix-mas
These vascular plants need liquid water to reproduce.

50,000
SPECIES OF FUNGUS LIVE ALONGSIDE LAND-DWELLING PLANTS.

MOSS
Sphagnum sp.
Bryophytes are the simplest of all land plants.

Epiphytes

grow on plants or on some other supporting surface. Their anatomy includes secondary adaptations that enable them to live without being in contact with the soil.

Grasses

take advantage of long hours of summer daylight to grow and reproduce. Their stalks do not have reinforcing tissues to help them to remain erect.

STEMLESS SOW THISTLE
Sonchus acaulis
The flowers are sent up from a basal rosette of leaves..

SWEET VIOLET
Viola odorata
This plant's spring flowers have a pleasant scent.

Giants

Trees are distinguished by their woody trunks. As a tree grows from a tender shoot, it develops a tissue that gives it strength, enabling it to grow over 330 feet (100 m) tall. Trees are found in the principal terrestrial ecosystems.

360 feet (110 m)

THE HEIGHT REACHED BY SOME SEQUOIA SEMPERVIRENS—COAST REDWOOD TREES

CHESTNUTS
Castanea sp.

WALNUTS
Juglans sp.

BEECHES
Fagus sp.

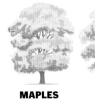

MAPLES
Acer sp.

OAKS
Quercus sp.

LINDENS
Tilia sp.

Anatomy of a Tree

The oak tree is the undisputed king of the Western world. It is known for its lobed leaves and the large cap of its acorn, a nut found on all trees of the genus *Quercus*. The tree's main trunk grows upward and branches out toward the top. Oaks are a large group, containing many types of deciduous trees. Under optimal conditions oaks can grow to a height of more than 130 feet (40 m) and live an average of 600 years.

The leaves absorb CO₂ and produce sugars by means of photosynthesis.

Transpiration (the loss of water vapor) in the leaves pulls the xylem sap upward.

CLIMATE
Trees grow in any place where there is sufficient water in the soil.

Flowers

The tree produces hanging male flowers, whereas female flowers are hidden among the leaves.

Buds

are formed by protective scales that fall off in the spring. They grow into new leaves and branches.

SUMMER
The oak blossoms. It increases in height, and its trunk grows thicker.

WINTER
The leaves fall away; the tree is dormant until spring.

SPRING
The cycle begins as the first leaves appear.

FALL
Low temperatures weaken the leaf stems.

Oak Products

The bark is rich in tannin, which is used in curing leather and as an astringent. The wood is strong and resists rotting, and is used to construct buildings, furniture, barrels, and, traditionally, ships.

ENERGY SOURCE
The chlorophyll traps energy from sunlight and uses it to convert water and carbon dioxide into food.

SURFACE
Mosses use the bark of oak trees as a source of moisture.

Roots

grow sideways to form a deep, broad root system.

Absorption of water and minerals

The xylem transports water and minerals from the roots to the rest of the tree.

The phloem transports sugars from the leaves to the rest of the tree.

Woodpeckers drill holes in the tree with their beaks as they look for insects.

Growth rings

Trunk

The trunk is strong and grows straight upward. The top of the tree widens with branches, which may be twisted, knotted, or bent.

Leaves

are arranged, one leaf to a stem, on alternating sides of the twig. They have rounded lobes on either side of the main vein.

SPRING
New leaves begin to replace the old ones.

WINTER
The leaves fall away, and the tree remains dormant.

FALL
The leaves stop making chlorophyll, and carotenoids and anthocyanins produce fall colors of red, orange, and bronze.

SUMMER
The leaves undertake photosynthesis, and the rest of the tree uses the sugars it produces.

Beginnings

In its first year of life an oak tree's roots can grow nearly 5 feet (1.5 m).

600 years

THE AVERAGE LIFE SPAN OF AN OAK

Achene: A hard seed that does not split open at maturity

Remains of the carpel (female reproductive part)

Seeds

Some species have sweet-tasting seeds; others are bitter.

Acorns

have dark stripes along their length. Their caps have flat scales.

Colors of Life

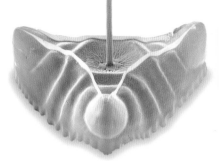

Algae are living things that manufacture their own food using photosynthesis. Their color is related to this process, and it has been used as a way of classifying them. They are also grouped according to the number of cells they have. There are many kinds of one-celled algae. Some algae form colonies, and others have multicellular bodies. Some types of brown seaweed can reach a length of more than 150 feet (45 m).

Mallomonas sp.

Single-celled Organisms

Many single-celled algae have flagella that enable them to move through the water. Most have the ability to ingest solid material through phagocytosis. Single-celled algae include some distinctive groups. Diatoms, such as the freshwater genus *Mallomonas*, are covered with a protective shell made of silica plates. Some single-celled algae, namely red algae, can thrive at relatively high temperatures. Red algae is unique among eukaryote organisms in its ability to live inside thermal water vents.

GREAT OPPORTUNISTS
Single-celled algae live near the surface of bodies of water. When they find an area with light and the nutrients necessary for development, they use asexual reproduction to multiply and colonize the area.

Fucus vesiculosus

Dictyota dichotoma f. *implexa*

1

Phaeophytes

are the 1,500 species of brown seaweed. They inhabit temperate regions and the rocky coasts of the coldest seas on Earth. Their color comes from the pigment fucoxanthin, a xanthophyll that masks the green color of their chlorophyll.

Dictyota dichotoma
(Hudson) J.V. Lamouroux

Cystoseira amantacea
var. *stricta*

*Ectocarpus
siliculosus*

Multicelled Organisms

This group of algae includes multicelled structures. They form colonies with mobile, single-celled algae that group together more or less regularly in a shared mucilaginous capsule. They can also appear in threadlike shapes, which branch off, or in bulky shapes, which are made up of layers of cells with a particular degree of cellular differentiation, that together are called a "thallus."

Micrasterias rotata

Scenedesmus quadricauda

Micrasteria staurastrum

Acetabularia crenulata

Pinnularia borealis

2 Chlorophytes

The majority of green algae species are microscopic, single-celled organisms with flagella. Others form into filaments, and yet others form large multicellular bodies. The group Ulvophyceae includes sea lettuce, which resembles salad lettuce and is also edible. The group Charophyceae includes stoneworts, which contain calcium carbonate deposits. The chlorophytes are linked evolutionarily with plants because they contain the same forms of chlorophyll, and their cell walls contain cellulose.

Chlamydomonas

6,000
DIFFERENT SPECIES have been classified within this group of green algae, or chlorophytes.

DISCOVERY FACT™

In the presence of excess nutrients, algae multiply very rapidly, creating algal "blooms" that can have harmful effects on ecosystems.

3 Rhodophytes

Red algae are characterized by their phycoerythrin pigments, which give them a reddish color by masking their chlorophyll's green. Most rhodophytes grow below the intertidal zone near tropical and subtropical coasts. They are distributed throughout the principal oceans of the world and grow mainly in shaded areas in warm, calm water.

Carrageenan red seaweed (*Chondrus crispus*)

Hypoglossum hypoglossoides

Bangia atropurpurea

Nitophyllum punctatum

Halymenia floresia

Apoglossum ruscifolium

Seeds, To and Fro

Reproduction from seeds is the most prominent evolutionary advantage in plants' conquest of the terrestrial environment. The seed shelters the embryo of the future plant with protective walls. The embryo is accompanied by tissues that provide enough nutrients for it to begin to develop. Optimal temperature and an appropriate quantity of water and air are the factors that stimulate the seed to awaken to a marvelous cycle of development and growth that will culminate in the generation of new seeds.

 AWAKENING OF THE SEED
Seeds, such as those of the field, or corn, poppy (*Papaver rhoeas*), leave their latent stage when they hydrate and receive enough light and air. Their protective coverings open and the embryo grows, thanks to the energy provided by its cotyledons, or seed leaves.

 TROPISM
Because of gravity, amyloplasts are always located in the lower part of cells. They produce a stimulus that encourages the root to grow toward the earth, a process called "geotropism."

Cell multiplication allows the stem to grow.

PLUMULE
The bud of a plant embryo that will produce the first shoot.

COTYLEDON
The first embryo leaf. It provides the energy needed for growth.

ABSORBENT HAIRS
These organs begin to develop in the radicle. They help the seed absorb water from the soil.

HARD COVER
Called the "testa," it can appear in very different forms.

RADICLE
The embryo root that will produce the main root of the plant.

The testa protects the embryo and the cotyledons during the seed's latent stage.

WATER
is responsible for breaking open seed covers because the hydrated tissues exert pressure on the interior of the seed.

NUTRIENTS
The radicle is in charge of collecting water and nutrients present in the soil.

Enzymes

Nutrients

ENDOSPERM

Gibberellin

Embryo

Seed cover

Gibberellins

During the first stages of germination following water absorption, these plant hormones are distributed through the endosperm. Their presence promotes the production of enzymes that hydrolyze starches, lipids, and proteins to turn them into sugars, fatty acids, and amino acids, respectively. These substances provide nutrition to the embryo and later to the seedling.

Fall

THE TIME OF THE YEAR IN WHICH THE SEED OF *PAPAVER RHOEAS* GERMINATES

GROWTH
The seedling grows and breaks through the surface. This causes the plant to be exposed to light so it can begin to carry out photosynthesis. It thus begins to manufacture its own nutrients to replace those provided by the cotyledons.

VEGETATIVE GROWTH
The first true leaves unfold above the cotyledons, and the stem elongates from formative tissue called the "meristem," located at the apex of the plant. Continued growth will lead to the formation of an adult plant, which will develop its own reproductive structures.

FLOWERING
Internal and external changes stimulate the apical bud to develop a flower.

APICAL GROWTH
Light stimulates the multiplication of cells in the apex of the stem.

The cotyledon is carried by the vertical growth of the stem.

Cotyledons can remain under the soil or, as in this case, grow above the ground.

HYPOCOTYL
The first part of the stem emerges and develops in the young plant.

TOTIPOTENCY
Characteristic of the vegetative apex cells.

SEED LEAVES

SESSILE LEAVES
The upper leaves have no petiole.

5 PRODUCTION OF THE FLOWER'S PARTS
The apical bud begins to produce fertile flower structures (gynoecium and androecium) and sterile structures (petals and sepals). The flower bud forms.

CONDUCTION
The stem carries water and minerals from the root to the leaves, while taking manufactured substances in the opposite direction.

0.4 inch
(1 cm)
IS THE MAXIMUM HEIGHT IT CAN GROW IN ONE DAY.

TRUE LEAVES

SECONDARY ROOTS

The root has many fine hairs that create a large surface area for water absorption.

PRIMARY ROOT
It anchors itself to the ground and branches out to support the plant in the substrate.

DISCOVERY FACT™
Some seeds can remain dormant for many years, or even for centuries, until conditions become favorable for germination.

THE FIRST 20 DAYS OF A FIELD POPPY

0.04 in (1 mm)   3 in (8 cm)   5 in (12 cm)   6 in (15 cm)   8 in (20 cm)

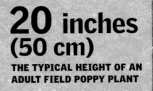

20 inches
(50 cm)
THE TYPICAL HEIGHT OF AN ADULT FIELD POPPY PLANT

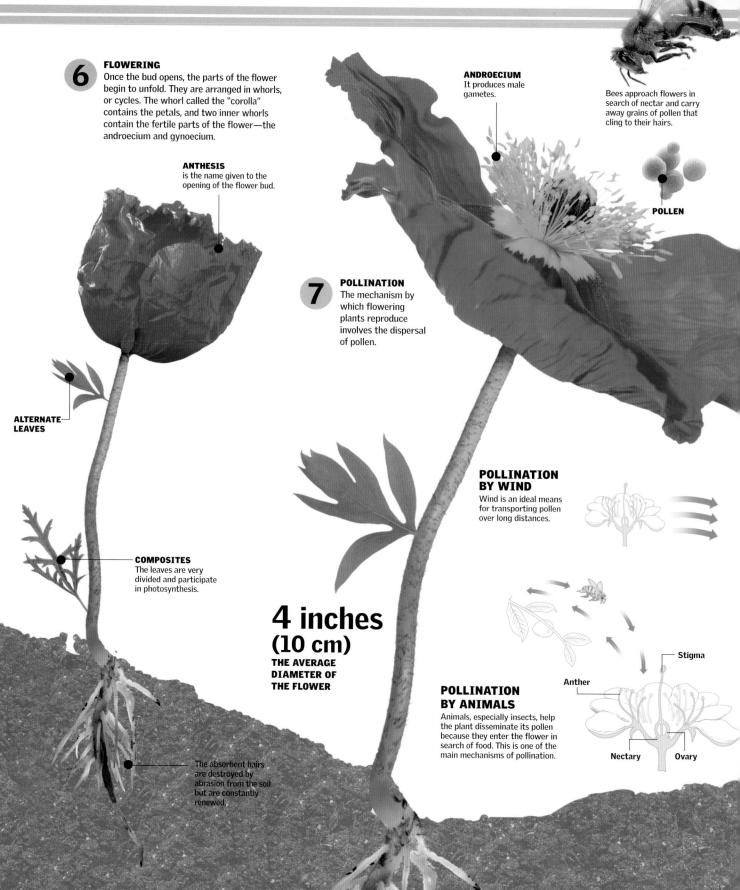

6 **FLOWERING**
Once the bud opens, the parts of the flower begin to unfold. They are arranged in whorls, or cycles. The whorl called the "corolla" contains the petals, and two inner whorls contain the fertile parts of the flower—the androecium and gynoecium.

ANTHESIS
is the name given to the opening of the flower bud.

ALTERNATE LEAVES

COMPOSITES
The leaves are very divided and participate in photosynthesis.

The absorbent hairs are destroyed by abrasion from the soil but are constantly renewed.

ANDROECIUM
It produces male gametes.

Bees approach flowers in search of nectar and carry away grains of pollen that cling to their hairs.

POLLEN

7 **POLLINATION**
The mechanism by which flowering plants reproduce involves the dispersal of pollen.

POLLINATION BY WIND
Wind is an ideal means for transporting pollen over long distances.

4 inches
(10 cm)
THE AVERAGE DIAMETER OF THE FLOWER

POLLINATION BY ANIMALS
Animals, especially insects, help the plant disseminate its pollen because they enter the flower in search of food. This is one of the main mechanisms of pollination.

Stigma

Anther

Nectary

Ovary

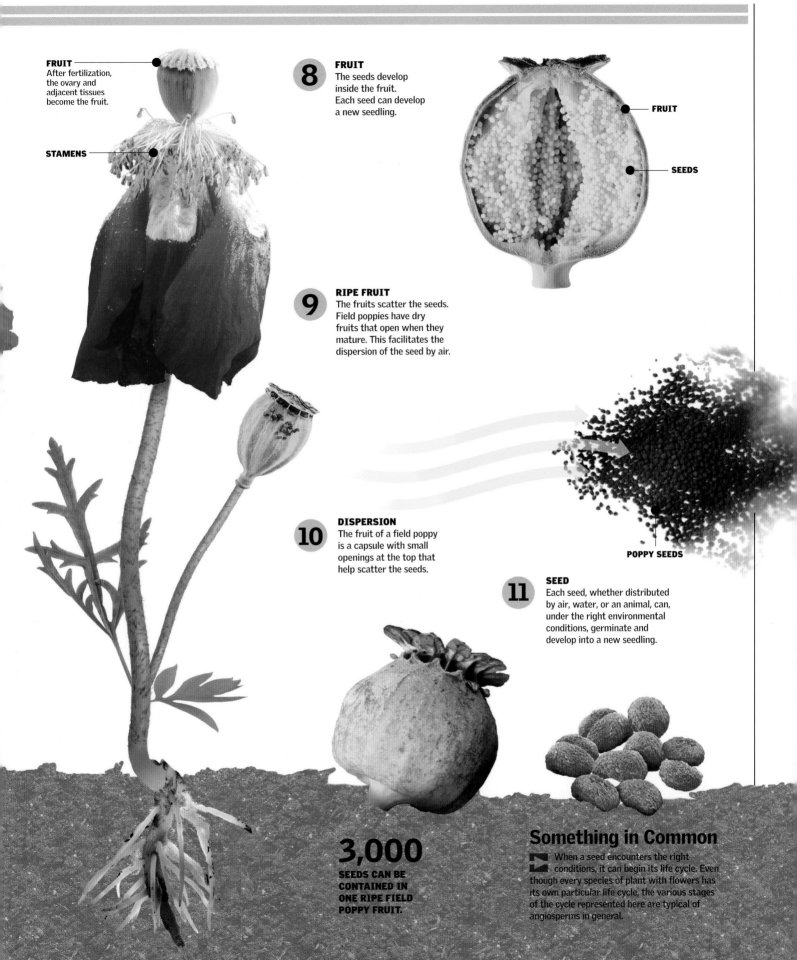

FRUIT
After fertilization, the ovary and adjacent tissues become the fruit.

STAMENS

8 **FRUIT**
The seeds develop inside the fruit. Each seed can develop a new seedling.

FRUIT

SEEDS

9 **RIPE FRUIT**
The fruits scatter the seeds. Field poppies have dry fruits that open when they mature. This facilitates the dispersion of the seed by air.

10 **DISPERSION**
The fruit of a field poppy is a capsule with small openings at the top that help scatter the seeds.

POPPY SEEDS

11 **SEED**
Each seed, whether distributed by air, water, or an animal, can, under the right environmental conditions, germinate and develop into a new seedling.

3,000
SEEDS CAN BE CONTAINED IN ONE RIPE FIELD POPPY FRUIT.

Something in Common
When a seed encounters the right conditions, it can begin its life cycle. Even though every species of plant with flowers has its own particular life cycle, the various stages of the cycle represented here are typical of angiosperms in general.

Pollination

The orchid, whose scientific name *Ophrys apifera* means "bee orchid," is so-called because of the similarity between the texture of its flowers and the body of a bee or wasp. Orchids' flowers are large and very colorful, and they secrete a sugary nectar that is eaten by many insects. The orchid is an example of an "entomophilous" species; this means that its survival is based on attracting insects that will transport its pollen to distant flowers and fertilize them.

ODOR
The odor is similar to bee pheromones.

CAUDICLE
At times it closes, covering the pollinia.

POLLINIUM
A small clump of closely packed pollen grains.

1
Attraction
When a flower opens, a liquid drips on its lower petal and forms a small pool. The liquid gives off an intense aroma that attracts male bees and wasps.

POLLINATING INSECT
Male solitary wasp, *Gorytes* sp.

3
The load
While passing through the narrow tunnel, the insect brushes the pollinarium, and pollen sticks to its body.

2
The fall
Excited by the perfume and the texture, the insect enters the flower, and in this pseudo-copulation it usually falls into the pool and becomes trapped. It cannot fly and can only escape by climbing the flower's stamens.

NECTAR
A sugary liquid that is somewhat sticky.

Bee Orchid
Ophrys apifera

LABELLUM
Its form imitates the abdomen of the insect.

POLLINIA
Small clumps
of pollen grains
are housed in a
compartment of
the anther.

0.008–
0.08 INCH
(0.2–2 MM)

POLLINARIUM
A grouping of two, four,
six, or eight pollinia.

GRAIN OF
POLLEN

Pollen

Each grain contains a male gamete.

12,000

**THE NUMBER OF SEEDS
THAT A SINGLE FERTILIZED
ORCHID CAN PRODUCE**

CORBICULUM
Some bee species have corbicula, or
pollen baskets, on their hind legs for
the transportation of pollen.

COLORATION
is one of the
factors of
attraction.

4

Transfer

The insect takes off
toward other flowers,
with pollen from the
orchid stuck to its body.

LOBULES
They have
fine, silky hairs
that attract
the pollinating
insects.

5

Toward a destination

When it arrives at another
flower of the same species,
the insect repeats the
incursion and bumps the
flower's stigmas (female
organs), depositing pollen
that is capable of fertilizing
the flower.

CAMOUFLAGE
Some plants that rely on insects for
pollination acquire the appearance
of the animal species on which they
depend for survival. Each orchid has
its own pollinating insect.

Energy Manufacturers

The main function of leaves is to carry out photosynthesis. Their shape is specialized to capture light energy and transform it into chemical energy. Their thinness minimizes their volume and maximizes the amount of surface area that is exposed to the Sun. However, there are a great many variations on this basic theme, which have evolved in association with different types of weather conditions.

EDGES (MARGINS)
Species are distinguished by a wide variety of edges: smooth, jagged, and wavy.

VEINS
Flowering plants (angiosperms) are often distinguished by the type of veins they have: parallel veins in monocots and branching veins in dicots.

PRIMARY VEINS
The products of photosynthesis circulate through the veins from the leaves to the rest of the body.

LEAF SURFACE
Colorful, usually green, with darker shades on the upper, or adaxial, side. The veins can be readily seen.

RACHIS

LEAF STEM (PETIOLE)

ACER SP.
This genus includes trees and shrubs easily distinguishable by their opposite and lobed leaves.

Simple Leaves

In most monocotyledon plants the leaf is undivided. In some cases it may have lobes or notches in its side, but these divisions do not reach all the way to the primary vein of the leaf.

Compound Leaves

When the leaf is divided from the primary vein, it forms separate leaflets. A compound leaf is called "palmate" when the leaflets are arranged like the fingers on a hand and "pinnate" when they grow from the sides of the leaf stem like the barbs of a feather.

CROSS SECTION
Generally, in cross section, it can be seen that a leaf possesses the same tissues as the rest of the body of the plant. The distribution of tissues varies with each species.

CONDUCTING TISSUE
is made of live cells (phloem) and dead cells (xylem).

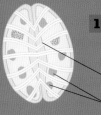

1 The stomatic apparatus is closed. No air can enter or leave the leaf. This prevents excessive transpiration, which could damage the plant.

Thickened cell walls in the area of the pore

Cellulose microfibers

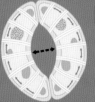

2 The stomatic apparatus is open. The stomatic cells are swollen. As tension increases, the cellular form is modified and is able to exchange gases.

PLANTS AND THE ENVIRONMENT
The flow of carbon dioxide and water vapor between the plant and the environment is essential for the photosynthetic process. This exchange can be affected by internal or external factors, such as changes in light, temperature, or humidity. In response to these stimuli, the stomas can open or close.

BASIC TISSUE
is formed by live cells that give structure to the leaf and usually contain some chloroplasts.

EPIDERMAL TISSUE
is composed of live cells. It surrounds all the parts of the leaf and the plant. It produces a substance that forms the cuticle.

DISCOVERY FACT™

When they stop producing chlorophyll in the fall, deciduous trees shed their leaves to reduce water loss and wind damage during the winter.

Change and Its Advantages

Conifers possess an interesting modification in their leaves. In these gymnosperms, evolution directed the abrupt reduction of surface foliage area. This gave them an adaptive advantage over plants whose leaves have a large surface area: less resistance to wind and less transpiration in arid climates. In addition, they are able to avoid the excessive weight that would result from the accumulation of snow on large leaves.

TENDRILS
The leaves of climbing plants, such as the grapevine, have these adaptive modifications.

VASCULAR BUNDLE
Formed by phloem and xylem

RESIN
functions to prevent freezing. It circulates through the resin ducts.

EPIDERMIS
Cells with thick walls and a thick cuticle

CONIFERS
Needle-shaped leaves are characteristic of conifers. They are usually oval or triangular. A hypodermis, which is enclosed by the epidermis, is broken only in the stomas.

GLOSSARY

Accretion Growth of an ice crystal in the atmosphere by direct capture of water droplets below 32°F (0°C).

Active Volcano Volcano that erupts at regular intervals.

Aftershock Small tremor or quake produced as rock settles into place after a major earthquake.

Air Mass Extensive volume in the atmosphere whose properties, in particular temperature and humidity in a horizontal plane, show only small differences.

Albedo A measure of the percentage of radiation reflected by a surface.

Algae Organisms of the Protist kingdom without roots, stems, or leaves. They live in water or in humid areas.

Angiosperms From the Greek *angion* (recipient) and *sperm* (seed). Plants with flowers whose seeds are contained in structures that develop into fruits.

Anther Structure of the stamen composed of ovaries and pollen sacs.

Anticyclone Region where the atmospheric pressure is relatively high, associated with good weather.

Aphelion The point in a celestial body's orbit farthest from the Sun.

Asexual Reproduction Process through which a single progenitor generates descendants identical to itself.

Asthenosphere Part of the Earth's upper mantle, below the lithosphere, composed of easily deformable rock.

Atmosphere Layer of gas retained around a planet by its gravity.

Atmospheric Pressure The pressure or weight exerted by the atmosphere at a specific point.

Aurora Luminous phenomenon, visible in the polar regions, caused by the collision of solar particles with the atmosphere.

Batholith Massive body of magma that results from an intrusion between preexisting layers.

Bryophytes Group of small flowerless plants, comprising the hepaticae, anthocerotae, and mosses.

Caldera Large depression left when a volcano collapses onto its magma chamber.

Canyon Deep, narrow valley formed by fluvial erosion.

Carbon One of the most common elements in the universe, produced by stars. All known life is carbon-based.

Carpel Female part that bears the ovules of a flower. The grouping of carpels forms the gynoecium.

Cave Subterranean cavity formed through the chemical action of water on soluble, generally calcareous, ground.

Cell Smallest vital unit of an organism.

Cellulose Fibrous carbohydrate that a plant produces as structural material, the main component of its cell walls.

Cementation Process by which sediment both loses porosity and is lithified through the chemical precipitation of material in the spaces between the grains.

Cementation Zone Place where lithification occurs. Water fills up the spaces between the grains of sediment, and transforms loose sediment into a solid mass.

Chemical Compound Substance formed by more than one element.

Chlorophyll Pigment contained in the chloroplasts of plant cells. It captures the energy of light during photosynthesis.

Chloroplast Microscopic sac, inside green-plant cells, where the chemical processes of photosynthesis take place.

Cirrus Wispy cloud formations at altitudes greater than 16,400 feet (5,000 m).

Clay Fine-grained sediment formed by the chemical decomposition of some rocks. Malleable when wet, it hardens as it dries.

Climate The average state of the meteorological conditions of a location considered over a long period, and determined by latitude, longitude, altitude, topography, and continentality.

Cloud A visible mass of small particles, such as droplets of water and/or crystals of ice, suspended in the air.

Coal Combustible black rock of organic origin, produced through the decomposition of plants in swamps or shallow waters.

Coalescence The process of growth of drops of water in a cloud. Two drops collide and remain joined after the collision, constituting a bigger drop.

Condensation Nucleus A small particle of dust or ash on which water vapor condenses during the formation of a cloud.

Contact Metamorphism Large-scale transformation of a rock into another type of rock, usually because of a sudden temperature increase.

Continentality The tendency of interior regions of continents to have more extreme temperature changes than coastal zones.

Convection The process by which a heated surface transfers energy to the material (air, water, etc) above it. This material becomes less dense and rises. Cooler material descends to fill in the void.

Convergent Boundary Border between two colliding tectonic plates.

Core The solid, high-pressure central mass of a planet.

Coriolis Force An apparent deflecting force that applies when the Earth is used as a reference frame for motion. It is strongest at the poles and does not exist at the Equator.

Cotyledon First leaf of flowering plants, found on the inside of the seed.

Crater Circular depression formed by the impact of a meteorite.

Crust Rocky layer of the surface of a planet or natural satellite.

Crystal Organized, regular, and periodically repeated arrangement of atoms.

Cyclone A climatic low-pressure system.

Cytoplasm Compartment of the cells of eukaryotes, marked by the cellular membrane and the membranes of the organelles of the cell.

Deciduous Describes a plant that loses all its leaves in specific seasons of the year.

Density Degree of solidity of a body (its mass divided by its volume).

Desert A hot or cold zone where annual precipitation is less than 1 inch (25 mm).

Dew Condensation in the form of small drops of water formed when the temperature has dropped to the dew point.

Dicotyledon Flowering plant whose seed has two cotyledons.

Dike A tabular igneous intrusion that crosses through layers of surrounding rock.

Earthquake A sudden and violent release of energy and vibrations in the Earth, generally at the edges of tectonic plates.

Eclipse Visual concealment of one celestial body by another. A lunar eclipse occurs when the Moon passes into the Earth's shadow, and a solar eclipse takes place when the Earth passes into the Moon's shadow.

Ecosystem Grouping of the organisms of a community and the nonbiological components of their environment.

Elliptical Orbit Orbit shaped like a flattened circle.

Embryo Product of an egg cell fertilized by a sperm cell; it can develop until it constitutes an adult organism.

Enzyme Protein that helps to regulate the chemical processes in a cell.

Eon The largest unit of time on the geologic scale.

Epicenter Point on the Earth's surface located directly above the focus of an earthquake.

Epidermis The external cellular layers of stems and leaves.

Epiphyte Plant that grows and supports itself on the surface of another plant but does not take water or nutrients from it.

Era Division of time in the Earth's history. Geologists divide eras into periods.

Erosion Action in which the ground is gradually worn down over long periods by moving water, glaciers, wind, or waves.

Evaporation Physical process by which a liquid (such as water) is transformed into its gaseous state (such as water vapor).

Exosphere The outermost layer of the Earth's atmosphere.

Extinct Volcano Volcano that shows no signs of activity for a long time, considered to have a very low probability of erupting.

Fault Fracture involving the shifting of one rock mass with respect to another.

Fertilization Fusion of the special reproductive cells (in the pollen and ovules) in order to give rise to a new plant.

Focus Internal zone of the Earth, where seismic waves are released, carrying the energy held by rocks under pressure.

Fog Visible manifestation of drops of water suspended in the atmosphere at or near ground level, reducing the horizontal visibility to less than a mile.

Fold Bending and deformation of rock strata due to the compression caused by the movements of tectonic plates.

Front The transition or contact zone between two masses of air with different meteorological characteristics, which almost always implies different temperatures.

Geology Study of the Earth, its shape, and its composition. Rocks, minerals, and fossils offer information that helps us reconstruct the history of the planet.

Germination Process in which a plant begins to grow from a seed or a spore.

Glacier A large mass of ice formed through the accumulation of recrystallized and compacted snow occurring either on a mountain or over a large area on a landmass. Ice moves slowly and both excavates rock and carries debris.

Gondwana Southern portion of Pangea, which at one time included South America, Africa, Australia, India, and Antarctica.

Granite Intrusive igneous rock composed mainly of quartz and feldspar.

Gravity Attractive force between bodies, such as between the Earth and the Moon.

Gymnosperm Plants with seeds that are not sealed in an ovary, such as conifers.

Gynoecium Grouping of carpels of a flower that make up the female sexual organ of angiosperms.

Hail Precipitation that originates in convective clouds in the form of masses or irregular pieces of ice. Strong upward currents are required inside clouds for hail to be produced.

Helium The second most common and second lightest element in the universe.

Hurricane A tropical cyclone with sustained winds of 64 knots (74 miles per hour [119 km/h]) or more.

Hydrogen The most common and lightest element in the universe; the main component of stars and galaxies.

Hyphae Interwoven filaments that form the mycelia of fungi.

Igneous Rocks Rocks formed directly from the cooling of magma, either inside the crust or on the surface as the result of a volcanic eruption.

Impermeable Rock Rock through which liquids cannot be filtered.

Incandescent A property of metal that has turned red or white because of heat.

Intrusion A large mass of rock that forms in empty spaces underground when magma infiltrates strata, cools, and solidifies.

Jet Streams Air currents high in the troposphere (about 6 miles [10 km] above sea level), where the wind velocity can be up to 200 miles per hour (90 meters per second).

Kingdom Taxonomic group superior to a phylum and inferior to a domain.

Lava Flow River of magma that flows out of a volcano and runs along the ground.

Light Electromagnetic radiation with a wavelength visible to the human eye.

Lightning A discharge of the atmosphere's static electricity occurring between a cloud and the ground.

Limestone Rock containing at least 50 percent calcite. It can also have dolomite, aragonite, and siderite.

Lithosphere Exterior, rigid layer of the Earth formed by the crust and upper mantle.

Magma Mass of molten rock deep below the surface, which includes dissolved gas and crystals. When magma has lost its gases and reaches the surface, it is called "lava."

Magma Chamber Section within a volcano containing incandescent magma.

Magnetic Field The area near a magnetic body, electric current, or changing electric field. Planets, stars, and galaxies have magnetic fields that extend into space.

Magnetosphere Sphere that surrounds a planet with a magnetic field strong enough to protect the planet from the solar wind.

Mantle Layer that lies between the crust and the core of a planet.

Marble Metamorphosed limestone rock composed of compacted calcite and dolomite.

Mass Measure of the amount of matter in an object.

Matter The substance of a physical object, it occupies a portion of space.

Meristem Region of tissue consisting of cells that produce other cells through cellular division.

Mesosphere The layer of the Earth's atmosphere that lies above the stratosphere.

Metal Any element that shines, conducts electricity, and is malleable.

Metamorphic Rock Type of rock resulting from the application of high pressure and temperature on igneous and sedimentary rocks.

Meteorite Rocky or metallic object that strikes the surface of a planet or satellite, where it can form a crater.

Meteorology The science and study of atmospheric phenomena.

Mid-Ocean Ridge An elongated mountain range on the ocean floor.

Mineral Inorganic solid of natural origin that has an organized atomic structure.

Molecule Smallest unit of a pure substance that has its composition and chemical properties. It is formed by one or more atoms.

Monocotyledon Flowering plant with only one cotyledon. Examples are the onion, orchid, and palm.

Mycelium Interwoven mass of hyphae of a fungus.

Nectar Sweet liquid, produced by flowers and some leaves, that attracts insects and birds, which serve as pollinating agents.

Neutron Electrically neutral subatomic particle. It makes up part of an atom's nucleus (except in ordinary hydrogen).

Node Axillary bud, the part of the stem of a plant where one or more leaves appear.

Ocean Current The movement of water in the ocean caused by the system of planetary winds. Ocean currents transport warm or cold water over long distances.

Ovary The part of a flower consisting of one or more carpels and containing the ovules. Fertilized, it will form all or part of the fruit.

Oxygen Chemical element vital to life, making up 21 percent of the Earth's atmosphere.

Ozone Layer A layer of the atmosphere 20–30 miles (32–48 km) above the Earth's surface between the troposphere and the stratosphere. It filters ultraviolet radiation.

Perihelion The point in a celestial body's orbit closest to the Sun.

Permeable Layers Strata of the Earth's crust that allow water to filter through.

Phloem Vessels that conduct the sap throughout the entire plant.

Photosynthesis Process through which light is used to produce carbohydrates from carbon dioxide and water.

Plate Tectonics Theory that the Earth's outer layer consists of separate plates that interact, causing earthquakes and forming volcanoes, mountains, and the crust itself.

Pollen Fine powder of plants with seeds whose grains contain the male sexual cells.

Pollination Passage of pollen from the male organ of a flower to the female organ of the same flower or another.

Precipitation A liquid or solid, crystallized or amorphous particle that falls from a cloud and reaches the ground.

Pyroclastic Flow Dense, hot mixture of volcanic gas, ash, and rock fragments that flows rapidly down the sides of a volcano.

Quartzite Hard metamorphic rock formed by the consolidation of quartz sandstone.

Radiation The process by which energy propagates through a specific medium (or a vacuum) via wave phenomena or motion. Electromagnetic radiation, which emits heat and light, is one form. Other forms are sound waves.

Rhizome Horizontal subterranean stem.

Richter Scale Measures the magnitude or energy of an earthquake. The scale is logarithmic, so that an earthquake of magnitude 8 releases ten times as much energy as a magnitude 7 quake. An earthquake's magnitude is estimated based on measurements taken by seismic instruments.

Rock
Natural aggregate of minerals (sometimes including noncrystalline substances) that constitute an independent geologic unit.

Root Organ that fixes a plant to the soil and absorbs water and minerals from it.

Sap Liquid that contains the products of photosynthesis, transported by the phloem.

Sedimentary Rock Rock that forms through accumulation of sediments that, when subjected to physical and chemical processes, result in a compacted and consolidated material.

Seedling First sprouting of the embryo of a seed, with a short stem and a pair of leaves.

Seismic Wave Wavelike movement that travels through the Earth from an earthquake or explosion.

Sepal Modified leaf that forms the outer covering of a flower.

Sexual Reproduction Reproduction based on the fertilization of a female cell by a male cell; it produces descendants different from both progenitors.

Shield Volcano Large volcano with sloping flanks formed by fluid basaltic lava.

Silicon One of the most common materials, a component of many minerals.

Slate Fine-grained metamorphic rock. It can be easily divided into sheets.

Snow Precipitation in the form of white or transparent frozen ice crystals, often in the form of complex hexagons.

Spore Reproductive structure formed by one cell, capable of originating a new organism without fusing with another cell.

Stamen Element of the male reproductive apparatus of a flower that carries pollen.

Stigma Upper part of a flower's female reproductive apparatus. The receptor of pollen, it connects with the ovary.

Stratosphere The layer of the atmosphere situated above the troposphere.

Stratus Low clouds that form layers. They often produce drizzle.

Subduction Zone Long, narrow region where one plate of the Earth's crust is slipping beneath another.

Tectonic Plates Large, rigid sections of the Earth's outer layer, which sit on top of a more ductile and plastic layer of the mantle and drift slowly at an average rate of 1 inch (2.5 cm) or more per year.

Thrust Fault A fracture in rock layers that is characterized by one boundary that slips above another at an angle of less than 45 degrees.

Tide The effect of the gravitational pull of one astronomical object on the surface of another.

Tissue Group of identical cells with the same function.

Tornado A column of air that rotates with great violence, stretching between a convective cloud and the surface of the Earth. Tornadoes can occur, under the right conditions, anywhere on Earth, but they appear most frequently in the central United States, between the Rocky Mountains and the Appalachian Mountains.

Transform Fault Fault in which plate boundaries cause friction by sliding past each other.

Tremor Seismic event perceived on the Earth's surface as a shaking of the ground, without causing damage or destruction.

Tropical Cyclone A cyclone without fronts, it develops over tropical waters and has a surface circulation organized in a counterclockwise direction.

Troposphere The layer of atmosphere closest to the ground, where most changes in weather take place.

Tsunami Word of Japanese origin for a large ocean wave caused by an earthquake.

Van Allen Belt Radiation zone surrounding the Earth, where its magnetic field traps solar particles.

Vascular Describes plants with a complex structure and highly organized cells for transporting water and nutrients to all parts of the plant.

Volcano Mountain formed by lava, pyroclastic materials, or both.

Weather The state of the atmosphere at a given moment, as it relates to its effects on human activity. It involves short-term changes in the atmosphere, in contrast to climate, which implies long-term changes.

Weathering The breaking down of a material by sustained physical or chemical processes.

Xylem Part of a plant's vascular system. It transports water and minerals from the roots to the rest of the plant.

INDEX

A

accretion, 16
adaptation, 77
African Plate, 31
albedo, 32–33
algae, 7, 59, 60, 68–69
algal blooms, 69
alluvial plain, 54
Alpine orogeny, 23
Alps, 16, 26
Andes, 16
angiosperms 61
animals, remains of, 58–59
aphelion, 11
aquatic plants, 62–63
Arabian Plate, 31
Archean eon, 17
ash, volcanic, 33, 59
Atlantic Ocean, 21
atmosphere, 7, 19, 32
atmospheric pressure, 36–37
autotrophy, 60

B

bacteria, 59
beach formation, 55
biosphere, 32
bryophytes, 60

C

caldera, 24
Caledonian orogeny, 22, 56
camouflage, 75
canyons, 52
Caribbean Plate, 30
cataclasites, 56
cementation process, 55
cereals, 61
Chinook wind, 42
chryosphere, 33
chlorophyll, 60, 77
chloroplasts, 60
cities, 43
cliffs, 54
climate, 5–6, 34–35, 42–43, 58
    zones, 34–35
climatic system, 32–33
clouds, 9, 40, 44-45, 48–49
coastal areas, 42
coastal drift, 55
coastal plain, 55
coastal wind, 43
Cocos Plate, 30
cold climate, 35
cold front, 38
compaction, 55
condensation, 9, 40, 44
condensation nuclei, 44
conifers, 61, 77
contact metamorphism, 57
continental drift, 20
continental shelf, 18, 55
continentality, 43
Coriolis force, 36, 38
cotyledon, 70
crops, 58
cryosphere, 33
cumulonimbus clouds, 48
cycads, 61

D

delta formation, 54
desert, 34, 52, 58
dew, 46
dunes, 52
dynamic metamorphism, 56

E

Earth, 9
    crust, 18, 20, 22–23, 56
    formation, 16
    movements, 10
    orbit 8, 10–11
    structure, 8–9, 18–19
earthquakes, 5, 16, 26–27, 30–31
    risk areas, 30–31
earthworms, 59
eclipses, 14–15
    calendar, 15
electrical storm, 48–49
epiphytes, 65
equinox, 10
erosion, 4, 52, 58–59
erratics, 53
estuary, 55
evaporation, 8, 40
exosphere, 19

F

fall, 10, 67
fault lines, 30–31
ferns, 60, 64
ferrel cell, 36
flowers, 7, 61
folding events, 16, 22–23, 26
forests, 7, 43
Franklin, Benjamin, 49
frost, 47
fungi, 6, 59, 60, 61
fusion of rocks, 57

G

gas exchange, 64
geology, 4
geotropism, 70
gibberellins, 70
gingko, 62
glacial cirque, 53
glaciers, 17, 53, 54, 58
gneiss, 56
Gondwana, 20
GPS technology, 21
grasses, 65
gravel, 58
gravity, 9, 12
greenhouse effect, 33
Greenwich meridian, 11
gymnosperms, 61

H

Hadley cell, 37
hailstones, 47, 48
heat islands, 43
Hercynian orogeny, 22
Himalayas, 23
hoar frost, 47
horsetail rushes, 60
Houston, Texas., 34
humus, 59
hurricanes, 50–51
    classification, 51
hydrologic cycle, 40–41
hydrometeors, 46
hydrosphere, 32, 40–41

I

ice, 8, 46, 48, 53
igneous rock, 59
insect pollinators, 72, 74–75
isobars, 38

J

Japan, 26, 28
jet lag, 11
jet stream, 37, 38
Jupiter, 9

K

Köppen climate classification, 35

L

laterite, 58
latitude, 11
Laurentia, 17
lava, 24
leaves, 76
Lhasa, Tibet, 35
lightning, 48–49
    lightning rod, 49
lithosphere, 19, 33
longitude, 11
lunar eclipse, 15

M

magma, 20, 21, 24–25, 57
magnetism, 4, 9
Manaus, Brazil, 34
Mariana trench, 30
Mars, 8
meanders, 54
Mercury, 8
mesosphere, 19
metamorphic rock, 56–57, 59
meteorite collision, 17
microorganisms, 58, 68–69
mid-ocean ridges, 18, 31
Moon, 4, 8, 12–13, 17
    eclipse, 15
    effect on tides, 12
    landscape, 13
    movements, 12
    phases, 13
moraines, 53
Moscow, Russia, 35
mosses, 60, 64
Mount Rainier, Washington
    State, 47
mountains, 18, 22–23, 42
mylonites, 56

N

nebular hypothesis, 16
New Zealand, 27
New Zealand Fault, 30

O

oak (*Quercus* sp.), 66–67
occluded fronts, 39
oceans, 8, 16, 40, 42
orchids, 61, 74
orogenies, 22–23

P

Paleozoic era, 16
Pangaea, 16, 20
particulates, 44
perihelion, 10
permafrost, 58
phaeophytes, 68
photosynthesis, 7, 64, 76–77
plants, 6–7, 60–67, 70–73
    reproduction, 70–73
plutons, 18
pneumatophores, 63
polar cell, 37
pollen, 7
pollination, 7, 72, 74–75
poppy (*Papaver rhoeas*), 70–73
precipitation, 32, 44–47
Proterozoic eon, 17
Protista, 60
pyroclastic material, 59

R

rain, 9, 32, 34, 40, 44–45
rainforest, 34
rankers, 58
rapids, 54
rhodophytes, 69
river delta, 54
rivers, 41, 54
rock cycle, 59
rocks, 4, 54–57
Rodinia, 16
roots of plants, 64
Rossby waves, 38
runoff, 41

S

Sahara Desert, 52
sand, 52
Saros period, 15
satellite imagery, 38
schist, 57
Scotland, 56
seaweed, 68–69
sedimentary rock, 52, 59
sedimentation, 54
seeds, 7, 61, 70, 73
    dormancy, 71
slate, 57
smoke, 33
snow, 46–47
"snowball Earth," 17
snowflakes, 46
soil, 7
    formation, 58–59
solar eclipse, 14–15
solar radiation, 4, 8–9, 32
solar wind, 9
solstice, 11
spring, 10, 67
stationary fronts, 39
storms, 48–49
stratosphere, 19
subduction zone, 20
submarine landslides, 29
summer, 10, 67
Sun, 8, 14, 33
    influence on tides, 12

T

taiga, 35
tectonic plates, 20–21, 22
temperate zone, 34
temperature distribution, 42
Theia, 17
thermosphere, 19
thunder, 48

U

underground circulation, 33
United States, 43, 51

V

valleys, 54
Van Allen belt, 9
Venus, 8
volcanoes, 5, 17, 24–25, 33

W

warm fronts, 39
water, 4, 8, 40–41, 62–63, 70
water vapor, 40, 44
weather, 5–6
weather fronts, 38–39
weather systems analysis, 37
weathering, 4
Wegener, Alfred, 20
wetlands, 62–63
whirlwinds, 42
wind, 32, 36–39, 42–43
winter, 10, 67

tides, 4, 12–13
till, 53
Timbuktu, Mali, 35
time, 10–11
time zones, 11
tornado, 50
Trade Winds, 36, 37, 50
transpiration, 40, 64
transportation of rock, 53, 54
trees, 7, 65–67
    deciduous, 76
tropical cyclone, 50
tropical zone, 34, 58
troposphere, 19
tsunami, 5, 28–29
tundra, 35